AF241805

A
Little Piece
of
Heaven

A Little Piece of Heaven

a book of blogs

Dick Huguley

Deeds Publishing | Athens

Copyright © 2021 — Dick Huguley

Published by Deeds Publishing in Athens, GA
www.deedspublishing.com

Printed in The United States of America

Cover design by Mark Babcock. Text layout by Ashley Clarke.

Library of Congress Cataloging-in-Publications data is available upon request.

ISBN 978-1-950794-63-8

Books are available in quantity for promotional or premium use. For information, email info@deedspublishing.com.

First Edition, 2021

10 9 8 7 6 5 4 3 2 1

A Little Piece of Heaven is dedicated to my family:
Joan, my Wonderful Wife (WW)
Monica, Dalton and Tyler
Chad, Leslie and Aliina
Trey, Hunter, Austin, Neah, Kaisa and Annika
(a.k.a. THANKA)

Acknowledgements

Friends who encouraged me to keep writing blogs, you know who you are. I am especially grateful to those who took time to respond in writing. Your comments are inspirational:

"… your blog brought tears to my eyes … it brought back the sweetest memories of such innocent times … "

"I was hooked from the first sentence … hooked on every sentence, every word, every laugh line, and even have been brought to tears … "

"It would be difficult for me to express how deeply this warms

my heart. The gratification I feel when someone appreciates us is overwhelming…"

"… Yes, I do believe in miracles…"

"Such a lovely story and you brought tears streaming down from my eyes…"

"Thanks for your encouraging story, reminding us God is always infused into our daily lives…"

"Multiple chain miracles in my opinion but given to a family worthy of divine intervention."

"This nails it… churches/congregations have really changed over the years…"

"Thanks for taking me back to my childhood that I loved!!!"

"And now I feel like I really know your mom (I like her)."

"You keep walking me down memory lane, and I'm sure enjoying the trip."

"You had me from the start. Felt like I was right there. Write on, brother!"

"I smiled the whole way through this one… love it!"

"You just brought from the deep corners of my mind so many wonderful memories … thank you for that, and you're right, we sure didn't need technology to have the time of our lives! I treasure those days and pray I'll always remember … "

"Love reading about your travels. And especially the people you met. Fascinated about the one that sees through the eyes of his wife … "

"Okay, so that one made me cry … "

" … should be required reading for anyone who wants to find a job and a career … "

"I laughed out loud just thinking about you guys laughing … "

" … I don't know how you did it with seven people in a one-bath house … "

"That was a tough one to read, but sweet, sweet memories none-theless."

"Your first of many books of riveting stories — keep writing."

Preface

I received an important gift on Christmas Day, 2017. My son Dalton gave me my own blog spot. I didn't really know what it was. When he called it a notepad, I started to get it. Then he made it clear that he was tired of waiting for the book I always had promised to write.

So, the website www.dickhuguley.com came into being, created by Dalton. He told me it would be good to name the blog spot, but I didn't know where to begin. What in the world would I write about—or blog about—and how did authoring a book relate? Broad topics that came to mind initially related to areas of most importance in my life: family, friends, church, career . . . and The Cabin (note the capitalization). All of these were wide-reaching topics that needed to be narrowed, which made my head spin. As usual, however, I was overthinking this thing. Just let it flow.

"A Little Piece of Heaven" was born December 28, 2017, with a picture of The Cabin as background. By early 2019, I had written and published 38 blogs with about 20 additional drafts simmering. "Published" can be misleading. I wrote my blogs through a service called WordPress and distributed them through a small email list and Facebook. No doubt, the most rewarding part of blogging has been receiving feedback from readers, many of whom were friends from my childhood, seldom-seen relatives, former teachers who were pleased to see that I used a comma in compound sentences, former newspaper and business colleagues, and, most importantly, my children and grandchildren. I included some of that inspirational feedback in the acknowledgements section of this book.

While the centerpiece of a lot of these blogs is The Cabin, I simply wrote as the subjects came to mind. When organizing materials for this publication, individual blogs seemed to relate naturally to one of five areas—not surprisingly the same areas that came to mind two years earlier: family, friends, church, career, and The Cabin. Thus, the structure of the book.

Despite encouragement to continue publishing blogs, especially from my WW, I had a Forrest Gump moment in early 2019 when I decided to stop distribution of the blogs. I was not tired of writing nor drained of topics; I just decided to stop—like Forrest did when he had run halfway around the world and decided on the spur of the moment not to run anymore. I continued to write and file away drafts, and several of those were developed into blogs and are included in this book.

"A Little Piece of Heaven" the book is intended as entertainment and perhaps enlightenment. It's a book of blogs. If you want a long novel that keeps you in suspense, you might want to put this back on the shelf. If you are a deeply serious person, you might want to read something else. But, if you want to crack a smile or chuckle, maybe even shed a soft tear, "A Little Piece of Heaven" just might be a good companion.

Introduction

I created a blog spot for my Dad because he's a brilliant writer, amazing man, incredible Dad and he's always told me he was going to write a book one day. Well, I'm tired of waiting so it's time he has a place to write … about whatever he wants … and I bet we'll enjoy it.

Time will tell but I suspect he'll do some writing from his lake house, maybe from his boat in the middle of Lake Sinclair, or possibly—just possibly—from his recliner in Woodstock.

I love you, Dad. Merry Christmas and enjoy your new notepad … I mean blog spot.

… from Dalton (December 25, 2017)

Table of Contents

1. The Cabin

The screened porch of The Cabin has been my best writing spot. Early morning, looking at the lake, listening to the birds, watching the animals, and thinking, thinking, thinking. Me, my iPad, a cup of coffee, and always a couple of spiders. Whether coming or going, chair rocking or grilling, relaxing or sweating, fishing or swimming, The Cabin always seems to sprout a tale or two. It's easy for your mind to wander and your body to rest. It's like a mancave in heaven. My WW says The Cabin has added at least 10 years to my life. Does that mean if I were to spend more time there, perhaps I would live longer? Maybe I'll give it a try.

A Little Piece of Heaven

It's only fitting that my first blog be about The Cabin. Regardless of what my WW (Wonderful Wife) might say, I do not love The Cabin more than her. And, I do not love it more than my kids and grandkids. Everything else in the world? Maybe so. Okay, probably so.

I wish everybody could have their own little piece of Heaven. My WW says it has added at least 10 years to my life. We've been married 47 years—my WW and me—and The Cabin and I will celebrate our 20th anniversary this year. About 19 years ago on a stressful day at work, I decided I needed a break. Told my secretary—you could call them that back then—I was gone. That was code for "to The Cabin." She knew where I was headed, but she didn't know when she would see me again.

So, I escaped. Just like that, I was gone. Even the Atlanta

traffic didn't slow me down. I do remember calling my WW on the way. She answered with, "You're on the way to The Cabin, aren't you?"

It's about a two-hour drive to my little piece of Heaven, but it seems like it takes six hours to get there. But even the drive whittles away the stress. The Cabin is in middle Georgia on a little-known lake. It's on about six acres and cannot be seen from the road. Those are the only directions you're going to get because it's wonderfully quiet there, especially weekdays, and I want to keep it that way. I once went for five days and four nights and didn't have to speak to anybody. Absolute bliss. My WW just cannot relate to that.

The Cabin became part of the family almost by accident. WW and I were in a boat with friends, motored into a cove and saw two large homes for sale. Those two homes were the opposite of my desire for a retreat—way too big, sprawling with sweeping decks, three levels of bedrooms. Nice but not for me. I already had a nice home in Roswell. Directly between these two homes, however, was a vacant lot loaded with trees. As our boat moved closer, I realized the vacant lot was not vacant at all. Nestled under the thick trees was a small log cabin. For Sale sign on the dock, and my heart started pumping. Twenty-four hours later, WW and I knocked down the spider webs and opened the front door. One look inside and we faced each other and said simultaneously, without a lot of hoopla, "This is it." Very soon after, it would join the family and become The Cabin.

The Cabin had been closed for about two years before being rescued. Squirrels had found their way inside, couldn't remember how to get out, and gnawed the wood around window-panes, apparently trying to escape. The gnawed windowpanes remain today; some things in this world just don't need to be fixed. Wildlife also made lunch of the cedar two-by-sixes on the lakeside porch, creating a nearly perfect semi-circle at the top of the steps leading to the porch. Some things in the world need to be fixed so that semi-circle soon disappeared, replaced by other full length two-by-sixes and a screened porch to keep the varmints at bay. But outside changes to The Cabin have been few and far between since then. After all, how do you improve on a little piece of Heaven?

And, about that day I left work in search of some time without stress? Well, I bought a dozen minnows at the four-way stop 6.5 miles from The Cabin, eased the jon boat into the lake, cranked the small 15 horsepower Merc, and anchored mid-cove. Opened a lawn chair in the jon boat for a bit more comfort as a slight breeze positioned the boat for a perfect view of The Cabin. Two hours later I gave a dozen minnows their freedom. I had leaned back, closed my eyes, and never even put the fishing lines in the water.

So it is at The Cabin.

Field Camera Fun

A new adventure at The Cabin. As if I needed one.

Nearby neighbors kept mentioning the big buck they see occasionally roaming near The Cabin. One sighting described the buck as "about a ten-pointer, maybe more; huge for this area." I kept an eye out for the prized deer, rolling slowly along the long driveway when arriving and departing. I would never want to bullseye the big buck but surely would like to see it.

Deer are not necessarily plentiful on the six-acre plot, but it's not unusual to see them, especially does and their underlings munching acorns near the circle driveway. They also like early morning dessert near the courtyard, usually the prettiest flowers planted by my WW. But seeing the 10-pointer was a challenge—still is. But I think I'm getting closer.

My friend Ronnie has 300 or so acres in a speck of Alabama called Pine Apple. His farmhouse and land make up his Little Piece of Heaven. Three RDH guys (me, namesake Dalton and namesake Trey) are fortunate to get an invitation each year to deer hunt on this oasis, which has to be considered the deer capital of the South. I do not hunt; I'm the cook. But Dalton, and especially Trey, have learned immensely from Mr. Ronnie about the right way to hunt—respect for the land, respect for wildlife, and utmost respect for safety.

On my most recent trip to Pine Apple, Ronnie enlightened me on his new practice—utilizing field cameras to track deer on his acreage. We stopped deep in the woods where he ejected a tiny SIM card from a small, camouflaged camera that was strapped to the trunk of a tree. He then inserted the card into a device and plugged the device into his I-phone. Presto, pictures from the night before suddenly appeared, some showing deer enjoying a midnight snack on one of his fields. Time, date, and temperature on each picture. He had me. Or, this field camera thing had me.

So, one trip later to Bass Pro Shop for a camera and attachments, and only one question remained: just how fast could I get to The Cabin? It didn't take long.

Once at The Cabin, in a rare act of patience, I actually read the instructions for setting up the camera. I wanted to get this right. I programmed it to snap one picture every two seconds for eight seconds each time movement was detected. In other words, I would get four pictures every time something moves within camera range. My confidence level about this programming stuff was not very high, so I decided an overnight test was in order.

The test included strapping the camera to a porch post so it would pick up any movement in the courtyard. The next morning, I was amazed that I had programmed the camera perfectly. I also was amazed to get 112 pictures of my oscillating sprinkler. Each time the water spray would enter the range of the camera … presto, four pictures … then four more … then four more. At least I knew the settings on the camera were correct. And, I knew the sprinkler system was working well, too.

I did not flinch at that minor distraction. Next step was to strap the camera to a tree in the woods. A gorge running through the property seemed like a logical place—surely deer would want to shelter there. And they did. Another placement another night snapped an unsuspecting red tail fox. And then there are squirrels, lots of squirrels, who often trigger the camera. One obviously was curious of that thing strapped to his tree. Got a good close-up of his eye.

So, the field camera has been tons of fun with good results. A favorite series of pictures shows a hawk landing, pouncing on a squirrel, and flying away with the squirrel clearly visible in his talons. Other animals on file include lots of deer, raccoons, a variety of birds, a disgustingly fat possum, a fox, and a cat—not sure if it is a bobcat or wildcat or just an ugly domestic kitty.

But, no big buck. Not yet.

Thought I Had Him

I had been waiting six months to see the big buck roaming near The Cabin.

My friend Jason had seen the buck a couple of times this year and didn't believe his eyes. Jason grew up in the area around Lake Sinclair in Georgia, and he knows very well the area between Twin Bridges and Old Plantation, both roads off Highway 212. Knows it as well as he knows each of his four sons.

"It's the biggest I've ever seen in this area," Jason said earlier this year of the buck. "Got to be at least an eight-point, but most likely a ten, maybe even more." This from a long-time hunter not prone to exaggerate. And my lake neighbor Bill confirmed a couple of sightings as well: "Eight-point or bigger."

So, it was January when I started strapping a trail camera to different tree trunks in the area, guessing where deer might move. The camera snapped many pictures of wildlife, including plenty of deer, but nothing close to an eight-pointer. Being basically a city-slicker—at least that's what my WW calls me from time to time—I was just guessing and using my city-slicker common sense when picking places for the camera.

Then, just a couple months ago, Jason gave me some rural country advice. "If you want to see deer, get a bag of corn," he said. "Toss a few handfuls out in the woods."

But that wouldn't be fair. I'd rather let nature take its course without introducing any artificial advantages. Then again, corn just might serve as an equalizer and be an offset to my city slickerness. After all, I wasn't going to shoot this big buck; I just wanted a picture of it. But I decided against a bag of corn.

As August approached, the buck was still winning this game, but I wanted a fair and legitimate victory. The camera was getting plenty of pictures of deer but mostly fawns and does and a couple of spikes. No big buck. I just needed patience.

Then, around the first of August, neighbor Bill, who lives full-time at the lake, mentioned he had been seeing a lot of deer, including bucks, on his property and mine. More deer than usual. Jason came by The Cabin, smiled, and repeated, "Get some corn."

I did not get a bag of corn. However, I started some serious rationalization. And then, before leaving The Cabin one weekend, I did my normal check of our refrigerator and noticed four ears of corn somewhat hidden in the vegetable bin. Surely this was a sign from above. I could carry that corn away with our trash to the nearby dumpster, or I could shuck it, cut it off the cob … and …

Well, four ears of corn equal two or three handfuls. When thrown in the woods it easily scatters. I mean, after all, deer need to eat. And corn is a vegetable, which means it is a healthy food. I also rationalized in a number of ways that the corn should be thrown in the woods in an area just in front of the pine tree on which the trail camera just happened to be strapped. So much for my sportsmanship and hunting ethics.

Upon arrival a week later, I unstrapped the camera and toted it into the cabin. The first few frames showed the usual — pest control guy was on time, yard service was punctual as always, neighborhood fox was right on schedule, and then … there it was … August 15, 2018, 6:01 AM … beautiful big buck, eight-point rack stretching high with The Cabin in the background as a bonus.

The saga should end there, but it does not. I texted several pictures of the buck to Jason and others. Jason came by The Cabin the next day with some bittersweet news: "That's a very nice eight-point in your picture, but it's not the one I've been seeing. No doubt about it after looking at the pictures. The big one, at least a ten-point, is still out there."

So, this city slicker is going to buy a bag of corn.

Those Georgia Power Guys

My intentions were good; my wallet was just a bit lighter.

The weather was worse than crummy. The skies were blackened, wind was whipping around, and the forecast warned to keep an eye open for possible violent storms. That forecast was for Woodstock.

By the end of the day, the weather front had spared Woodstock and surrounding areas but moved toward the sacred ground of middle Georgia. Sacred, of course, because middle Georgia is the location of The Cabin. Milledgeville, the first capital of Georgia, and Eatonton, known only for its Uncle Remus Museum, are often in the path of serious weather fronts, and nobody really knows why. But this was one of those days.

That day became night, and then news reports the next morning revealed that trees were down amid some damage in the Milledgeville area. Those reports most likely included the Lake Sinclair area where power lines are above ground and serve as magnets for aging trees. Then our lake neighbors called to say power was out. For most people, I guess, that would not be good news. For me, however, it was an opportunity to head to The Cabin. Just to check on things, of course. Even though the lights were out, the air conditioner was out, the stove was out—all reasons to stay away. Plus, you never know how long it will take those Georgia Power guys.

"Just go," my WW said with a tinge of exasperation. And that's all it took.

Before leaving, I rationalized that the cabin's refrigerators would need attention if the electricity was off an extended period of time—even though the upstairs refrigerator is left basically bare because of occasions like this. But the risk for the refrigerator downstairs in the Man Cave was much greater. That's where the freezer guards the fish caught in Sinclair—fish caught by grandchildren who would be devastated to learn their fish had to be taken to the local trash dump. "Of course," my WW deadpanned. "Just go."

So, yes, I easily convinced myself that it was important for me to make the trip. Sure, it was. But this would turn out to be a time I might should have stayed in Woodstock. Or left my wallet there.

Some limbs and trees were down as I turned into the long gravel driveway that afternoon at The Cabin, but no serious damage was in sight. The Cabin seemed a bit quieter with no electricity, a false impression; it's always quiet on weekdays. I also knew it would be pitch-black dark in The Cabin and around the cove without lights at night. And, you never know how long it will take those Georgia Power guys.

So, I was hunkering down and preparing for a long night. While it was still daylight, I made sure candles and flashlights were handy and the outdoor gas grill was in place to heat coffee the next morning. Media reports indicated power could be out for another 48 hours.

And then, at about 4 o'clock in the afternoon, the lights came on. The refrigerators started to hum. Ceiling fans started to spin. I turned on the TV for an update. Those Georgia Power guys had worked through the night and restored electricity to many areas, including some around Lake Sinclair. In a way, they had spoiled my fun, but the day was not done, and the Georgia Power guys were not done with me.

I chose Longhorn Steakhouse in Milledgeville for dinner. A lot of other people did, too. So, my only choice for seating was near the front, a booth where I could see others come through the front door. Of all things, two Georgia Power workers came in. They were dirty head-to-toe and obviously tired from a long day—and night—of work. As they trudged past my booth on the way to their seats at the back of the restaurant, I had a feeling of guilt about my earlier notions about Georgia Power guys. They actually had worked through the night so we could have our comforts sooner than expected. Hats off to them.

And then it occurred to me: the least I could do was pay for dinner for these guys. After a few minutes, I motioned for the Longhorn manager to come over. "The Georgia Power guys who came in earlier, would you arrange for me to get their bill … discretely, anonymously?" I asked.

"Of course," the manager said. "No problem."

I finished dinner, paid my bill first, and then waited until the server brought the bill for the Georgia Power guys. "Very nice of you to do this," the server said. "Very nice."

"It's the least I can do," I told the server. "Those guys worked hard for all of us. Please tell them after I leave and also thank them for their hard work."

Then I looked at the bill. The two workers had joined six other Georgia Power workers at a table for eight at the back of the restaurant. Which meant a bill for eight hungry workers.

Which meant $304 plus 20 percent gratuity. Which meant I nearly swallowed my breath mint on the way out the door.

Maybe I should have stayed in Woodstock. But I just smiled.

My intentions were good; my wallet was just a bit lighter.

Tornado? No Problem

When I first met Jason many years ago, I asked if he would take care of the yard at The Cabin. His answer was quick and short: No problem.

He didn't know what he was getting into. Since then, regardless of the situation, he has never flinched.

When the water heater busted and flooded the Man Cave, no problem. When The Cabin needed wiring for another light in the loft, no problem. When a deer died and decayed on the lakeside, attracting a flock of buzzards, no problem. When the green metal roof needed a bath, no problem. When the wash pump froze, the heating system went out, the huge trees needed to be removed, no problem, no problem, no problem. There's nothing Jason cannot do.

So, a year ago, a wicked tornado waited until I departed The Cabin before swooping down into the cove.

My ride back to Woodstock was two hours old, which meant I was only a couple of miles from home when my cell phone chirped. Lake neighbor Bill said the tornado had ripped off some boat house shingles, splintered some tall pines, and damaged some nearby homes. Trees, limbs, and debris everywhere so "you might want to come back and take a look."

Bill does not tend to exaggerate nor get excited about much. The only time I've seen him slightly pumped up is when he's explaining the next project for his lake house or talking about another new boat. He's a great neighbor who has not put down his hammer since moving in years ago. And, when Bill puts down his hammer for his cell phone, you can bet it's something important.

I had already tried to call Jason before I made a sharp U-turn. It would take two hours to re-run the roads back to

The Cabin. Radio reports were not encouraging. When big-city Atlanta radio mentions middle Georgia and Milledgeville, it can't be good.

It was unusual not to be able to reach Jason by phone. His house is about five miles from The Cabin, and I was concerned that it might have been hit by the tornado.

I worried about Jason and his family until I pulled up to The Cabin. There they were. In the two hours it took for my return, they had already completely cleared all trees and limbs, returned chairs and benches to the dock, raked up all debris, nailed down a heavy tarp over the damaged boat house roof, and carried off a ton of blown shingles.

Evan, six years old at the time, was toting a heavy load of damaged shingles when I arrived. A healthy 12-year-old would have trouble lifting that many shingles. Evan wasn't even breathing hard and had a smile on his face.

Evan (7), Bradley (11), and Bret (15) form quite a work crew with their dad. They will be glad when their other brother, two-year-old Ethan (aka "Red"), gets a little older so he can start shouldering his share of the workload. Folks in rural middle Georgia seem to possess a tough, get-it-done work ethic not experienced by city-slickers. They also have instincts to care about their neighbors and friends. Like on tornado day.

"We were worried about the cabin, so we all hopped in the truck and headed this way," Jason said. "Looks like the cabin is okay, but we couldn't see the ground when we got here. It was covered up."

For years, Jason's lone sidekick was Bret. Then Bradley

came along. Then Evan and it won't be long before Ethan fills out the work team. When you join this team, your first responsibility is to pick up sticks, limbs, and anything else and put them in the fire ring. Then, assuming you do a good job, you are promoted to the rake or blower and then to the edger. Once you achieve those levels, you might graduate to the riding mower. Only Bret has made it that far, but Bradley is close behind.

Watching these boys grow up has been a rewarding experience. Evan is strong and a hard worker. Mischief has found him on the job a couple of times. He likes to dig for worms—an understandable distraction back at age four—and he loves to fish, which he has learned is a fun thing to do but not when your job is picking up sticks and limbs. Bradley sometimes misses trips to The Cabin during baseball season; he likes to strut the bases after knocking the cover off the ball, which happens often. And Bret, the big brother everybody wants, quietly sets the good example for his brothers.

Jason is stern with all his boys, but the education they are getting is invaluable and not taught in most of today's classrooms and homes. Hard work. Listening. Discipline. Respect for elders. Yes, sir; no, sir. Yes, ma'am; no, ma'am.

And helping neighbors and friends comes naturally for these guys. Like on tornado day when The Cabin and grounds actually looked better than normal.

No problem.

Haunted Hamburgers

Rides to The Cabin can be fun.

Many times, I ride with Billy Joel or Rod Stewart or Neil Diamond. Maybe even Anne Murray or Jimmy Buffet or Dolly Parton. Music from the sixties never gets old.

But my best rides to The Cabin have been with grandkids. Trey and Neah make the long ride short.

When Neah was younger, she liked to play the "Count the Cows" game. You know it … Neah had one side of the road, her brother Trey had the other side. They keep count of any cows they pass on their side, but a dreaded cemetery means all cows have to be buried and you start over at zero. The one with the most cows at the end of the trip is the winner.

When Neah was much younger, she was known to change rules in route, often wanting to count any horses she might see on her side. Or dogs. Or cats. One trip she wanted to count birds and then trees. Neah is a competitor and doesn't like to lose at anything. And she's smart—it didn't take but one trip for her to figure out the cemeteries don't move, so the winner always is determined early when sides of the road are picked. She never lost when her friends were along.

But the interest in cow counting didn't compare with the interest in the gas station-turned-restaurant in Shady Dale.

Shady Dale is actually just a four-way stop on Highway 142, a shortcut to The Cabin. It's one of those don't blink towns. Boiled peanut man on the corner is the second largest business. Ranked first is Robby's and Cindy's, the old gas station with bars on the windows to keep goof-offs from stealing the burgers.

You can have a country breakfast or other dishes at Robby's and Cindy's, but a hamburger lunch with their fries is the specialty. The hamburgers and fries embarrass the Golden Arches, Wendy's, or any other mass producer. Well worth waiting until the burgers go on the grill at 11 a.m. As good as the burgers and fries are, the stories told about this joint might be better.

The grandkids call it the Haunted Hamburger Place, and the tales never get old.

There's the door inside with the DO NOT ENTER magic marker sign. Bodies are apt to be hidden in there. And then there's the dark hall down to the bathroom. Most times Neah makes her decision early: "I think I can hold it until we get to the cabin," she says.

Rumors have it that a decapitation took place near the Haunted Hamburger Place. That's just a rumor, of course. But, friends of the grandkids want to know all the gory details, which from one telling to the next might change. Grandad's memory isn't as good as it used to be.

The big guy at the counter, that's Robby, has the look of the tall guy on the Munsters. The petite lady barking orders to the cook, that's Cindy. It's pretty clear Cindy is in charge, especially when Robby is out on the road piloting his tractor-trailer rig. You're lucky if you get a booth, otherwise it's a picnic table inside or outside. Parking outside is not plentiful but whatever you do, don't block the dumpster. Learned that the hard way with an admonishment from Cindy. Thought I might be hauled off to

Shady Dale jail when she got finished with me. That true story also has become a tale that seems to grow with each telling.

Been passing through that four-way stop about 20 years; Trey and Neah maybe 10 years. It was just Robby's to begin with before Cindy got her name painted on the cinder block front wall to make it Robby's and Cindy's. Whatever the apprehensions about the place, Robby's and Cindy's has a lock on repeat business. Truckers, power company employees, farmers, landscapers—anybody who gets dirty hands daily—like to gather at this intersection of Highway 142 coming from Newborn and Highway 85 going to Monticello.

When you finish your burger and fries and tales, you still have 25 miles to The Cabin. And it never fails. When Highway 129 passes over Murder Creek, it's the same question. "Grandad, why is it named Murder Creek? And they get the same answer: "Trust me, you don't want to know."

That tale begins with a body seen floating in the creek.

Rides to The Cabin can be fun.

ZimSkillet and Good People

One visit and I knew these were good people.

Highway 142 has a pretty stretch in Georgia between Covington and Eatonton. It's also a shortcut to The Cabin, which means it's a valuable find. A welder friend who knows the area revealed the shortcut through back roads that saves four miles each way.

Whether going or coming from The Cabin, this stretch of highway is rolling relaxation that passes through two small towns, Newborn and Shady Dale. Shady Dale stepped up to the big time not long ago with the opening of its own Dollar General.

But this is about Newborn, a town that looks out for its own, and the Zimmermans, a family that believes in giving back.

You actually could cruise straight through Newborn without stopping as long as you slow down where the law enforcement vehicle is parked. That vehicle stays in its parking spot for months at a time—spider webs prove it—so it's a decoy. But you really don't want to speed in Newborn anyway. You might miss the town's newest enterprise—ZimSkillet. A little background...

I've slowed down through this town for many years, passing the pretty white church beyond the railroad tracks, the taxidermy place at the somewhat main intersection, and the gas station and manual car wash next to Lucy's Wings. And, I had noticed a small breakfast spot, the Biscuit Shack, but rarely saw any cars or customers there. It was closed every time I wanted to stop for a biscuit or whatever. I wondered how it stayed in business or if it even wanted to.

Then one day while crawling 25 in the 35-speed zone, I noticed some activity on the grounds of the Biscuit Shack. A big, black smoker grill was out front, and the miniature shack, no bigger than a matchbox, was getting a significant touch-up. A couple of weeks later, a shelter was being built over the smoker, and a homemade sign was advertising barbecue, tenderloins, and other items. The finishing touch was a simple street sign with the odd, new name: ZimSkillet.

The Biscuit Shack had been transformed into ZimSkillet, and it was open for breakfast and lunch and by-the-pound BBQ. One U-turn later and I was squeezing in the front door. The inside was bigger than it looked from the road, even had some tables for customer seating, and it was the proverbial beehive of activity. The kitchen area was about the size of a telephone booth (remember those?), and four people behind the counter were bumping elbows and loving every minute of it while preparing orders for customers. Everybody was smiling and laughing and having fun. While working no less.

The lady taking my order could tell I was a first-timer to ZimSkillet—surely a city-slicker with white tennis shoes and creased slacks and, no doubt, not one of the 749 Newborn residents. While helping with every detail of the menu, this lady also called every local by name as they entered. And she smiled. All the time. Like everybody in the place. Something special seemed to be going on in ZimSkillet, and I was getting more curious by the minute. Plus, what was with this ZimSkillet name anyway?

A few minutes later, I enjoyed the best tenderloin sandwich of my life while sitting in my vehicle and watching two guys at the smoker grill as the parking lot filled with customers. The two guys doing the grilling were laughing and obviously enjoying their role in all of this. I was nosy.

"So, tell me about ZimSkillet," I said to the older of the two at the grill.

"I'd love to," said Paul Zimmerman, who temporarily delegated the cooking to his son Joe so he could share his story. And soon I knew why this place was so special.

The Zimmerman clan—Paul, his wife Laura, and their six children—moved to Newborn in 1996. The couple built their own home "with our own four hands" off Pitts Chapel Road. Paul was in medical sales and Laura home-schooled their children. Life was good until just before Christmas 2010. That's when their house and all their possessions burned completely to the ground. "All of our Christmas presents were already bought…first time we had ever done that early," Paul reminisced. "We lost everything."

Everything, that is, except for a few of his collection of cast iron skillets. Having been involved in youth sports teams with his children, Paul often provided food at team gatherings. Food prepared outside like smoked ribs, tenderloins, burgers, hot dogs. He loved doing it.

"We had nothing after the fire," Paul continued, "but the people of Newborn brought us everything we needed. Bags of clothes, food, toys, shoes, jackets—I still have the Carhartt jacket somebody brought; it's my favorite now. The Newborn people were unbelievable. They provided all we needed."

The twists and turns in life continued. The Zimmermans eventually were able to rebuild their home—"this time with a contractor rather than our own hands"—after winning a battle with their insurance company and a representative from big-city Boston who learned quite a lesson in big-hearted Newborn. And, to boot, Paul's medical sales team was eliminated, leading to a somewhat frustrating job search.

"But this was always a dream," Paul said, motioning back to the smoker, the parking lot and restaurant. The Zimmermans bought the Biscuit Shack from Pat Jarvis, a former pitcher for the Atlanta Braves who was gone more than he was in Newborn. And they began to follow their dream. "It's my way of paying back the community," Paul said. "The people of Newborn took care of us. This helps us give back to them."

So, with his family, his dream, his skillets and a smile, Paul launched ZimSkillet. Like the cast iron skillets, the Zimmermans have survived the devastating fire and more. And the town of Newborn is better for it.

The ZimSkillet menu surely will put some weight on this city-slicker traveling on Highway 142 to and from The Cabin. Whether it's a breakfast of the Loaded Dough Biscuit or a lunch of the pork tenderloin sandwich or a pound of BBQ to be warmed at The Cabin, this place will always leave a good taste in your mouth—in more ways than one.

One visit and I knew these were good people.

Signs And Serious Stuff

It has to be a good sign to get a spot on the wooden doors leading into the Man Cave at The Cabin.

Kinda like, *Heaven Is a Little Closer In a Home By the Water.* Or, *Every So Often Go Where You Can Hear A Wooden Screen Door Slam Shut.* Or, *My Wife Says I Never Listen; At Least That's What I Think She Said.*

Friends and family have added to the collection hanging on the inside of the garage doors. If lucky enough to be allowed to enter this area, most folks like to pause for a quick read. But not everybody gets a pass into the Man Cave. Interior decorators, for example, have lifetime bans. You're likely to be disqualified, too, if you are wearing a necktie or a dress. Cry-babies have to straighten up before getting in.

Lots of important plans have been devised in the Man Cave. Usually with grandchildren. Like how to thin out the nuisance squirrel population that loves to gnaw at the cabin's corners. Or, how to improve our chances of catching a 30-pound catfish. Or, whether to use blindfolds when taking visitors to our secret fishing spots. Serious stuff.

Lots of schemes have been devised in the Man Cave, too. Schemes are different from plans. A scheme, for example, is like devising a way to sneak neighbor Bill's pontoon out of his boat house so he thinks it has floated away. Or, how best to use a rubber snake around the fire pit. Or, finding the best hiding place for bubble gum and chocolate so parents don't know you have it.

There's a man cave rule, however, that has earned two different spots on the doors, which means it is super important: *What Happens at The Cabin Stays at The Cabin.* Again, serious stuff. Just ask the grandkids. Some of these plans and schemes could get us in trouble. And have.

The collection of signs and sayings for the Man Cave goes back many years, and the doors are filling up. But there always seems to be a little nook or cranny for another. Most of the signs make a lot of sense. Such as ... *I Wasn't Born at The Lake But I Got There As Fast as I Could.* Or, *I'd Rather Be Lost at The Lake Than Found at Home.* Or, *Looking for High-Speed Internet Access? Then Why Did You Come to The Lake?*

And the philosophical signs carry really deep messages. Like, *We Don't Stop Laughing Because We Grow Old, We Grow Old Because We Stop Laughing.* And *I Hope My House Is Always Too Small for All My Friends.* Better still, *If A Man Says He Will Fix It, HE WILL! No Need to Remind Him Every Six Months About It!* Or a couple of favorites of the grandkids (and some adults), *I Can't Be Good All the Time* and, *I Laughed So Hard Tears Ran Down My Leg.*

Some are simple and to the point, but all seem to carry a message or make you think: *Home of the Free Because of the Brave; Keep Calm and Carry On; Our Slice of Heaven;* and, *Fish Stories Told Here.*

Some of the others can help keep trouble away. Like, *If at First You Don't Succeed; Try Doing It The Way Your Wife Told You.* That one has helped me lots in the past with my WW. And some signs address attitudes: *$5 Charge for WHINING* or *Complaint Department 100 Miles Away.*

Honestly, there's a lot of truth to some of the signs. Like, *Through These Doors Pass the World's Greatest Fishermen.* And *The Grill Master Lives Here with His Old Flame.* Or *Genuine Antique Person—Been There, Done That, Can't Remember.* Don't remember the smart aleck who sent that one.

Enough of this. *The Lake Is Calling and I Must Go.*

Dianne the Decorator

There's no way Dianne the Decorator could win.

I had resisted for years making any changes to the inside of

The Cabin. As far as I was concerned, everything was perfect. Nearly perfect.

Well, maybe the orangish-looking timbers were somewhat overwhelming when you first came in. And the table for the flatscreen was a bit rickety. No shelves or cabinets anywhere for storage or whatever. And, the kitchen. Well, the refrigerator was sort of in the way, and the orangish-looking counters had space underneath for pots and pans but no place for food or kitchen supplies. And the bedrooms had furnishings that I called antiques. My WW called them outdated.

Everything was perfect. Nearly.

So, enter Dianne the Decorator (DTD). After years of perfection inside The Cabin, our favorite—and only—decorator was summoned. But just for her opinion. DTD is the only decorating person I would trust in The Cabin. She even speaks decorating language that I understand.

"So, when it's finished, what would you want it to look like—one word?" DTD asked while gazing at the interior. "One word other than cabin."

Now, wait a minute. She's on my home turf and she already is on the offensive, taking the lead and making me feel uncomfortable. Interrogating me. Maybe this decorator thing was a bad idea.

"She's a decorator," my WW interjected. "Just answer the question."

"Lodge," is the best I could come up with, which was fine with DTD.

So, I asked for her first impressions. "Lot of orange," she

said quickly. "We need less orange." It was as though she didn't even hear me say, "I like the cedar look." She decided to ignore this topic and move on.

"I do NOT want to change the cedar countertops in the kitchen, and you know you are NOT allowed to go into the basement, right?" I admonished. "Even though there are a lot of good decorating things, that's a private area. Like a man cave. The only way you could go in there would be if I blindfolded you." DTD basically ignored that comment, too, but did ask, "decorating things?"

"Well, fishing stuff," was my quick answer. "And old fishing lures."

"We'll see," was DTD's only commitment.

All parties—especially my WW—thought it might be a good idea for me to get lost for two or three weeks and let Dianne do her thing. I needed a heavy tranquilizer at that point, thinking again that this was a bad idea. Besides, everything in The Cabin already was nearly perfect.

So, I retreated to our home in Woodstock where my worrying continued. Actually, it increased. What if DTD decided to paint the inside of The Cabin? Or put flowers on the table. Or hang modern art on the walls. Or ...

"You should quit worrying," my WW lectured. "Dianne has always done good work for us."

My WW probably was right. But this was like going to a new barber for a trim and worrying about getting your head shaved. Except your hair will grow back. Changes at The Cabin might possibly be irreversible.

After a few days in Woodstock, I wondered if I should take a quick trip to The Cabin to check on the progress, if that's the right word. "Just go," my WW said calmly, knowing there was no other option for me. "Just go." And I did.

My heart started beating really fast as I turned into the gravel driveway and spotted The Cabin's green metal roof ahead. No vehicles in the circular drive which meant I could inspect inside alone. At least they hadn't messed with the driveway or the front porch, I thought to myself. Right when I was telling myself to have a better attitude, I opened the front door.

A tornado had somehow hit inside. Furniture had been moved out, including the shiny dining area table and my vintage sofa that had survived numerous college dorm moves. And the black refrigerator was gone. Along with the stove. Plastic covered all of the wooden floors. Unopened boxes were stacked. The counters in the bathrooms had been ripped out. Probably used a chain saw. I needed to leave.

I walked out the front door, started my Highlander and drove back to Woodstock, the perfect candidate for road rage. A king-sized headache stayed with me for three hours. Then I learned DTD had called the day before and left a message that the renovation would be finished in a couple of weeks and I probably should not go to The Cabin for a while. The word "renovation" caused my headache to return.

The next two weeks are a blur. Not sure two complete weeks had ever passed without a trip to The Cabin. Then the call finally came from DTD about meeting her at The Cabin. She was finished. The deed was done. The big reveal awaited.

For whatever reasons, both DTD and my WW could not get to The Cabin as quickly as I could. After a restless night, I headed toward middle Georgia alone. I was sure to take a legal pad and pen so I could write down all of my suggestions, i.e., complaints.

When I pulled back the screen door, opened the old wooden door, and walked in … I immediately dropped the legal pad and pen. Didn't need it. Was this a page out of Southern Living or what?

I inspected The Cabin in awe. Built-in shelves with a pull-out and swivel flatscreen flanked the brick fireplace. A custom dining room table, hand-crafted from roughened wood, replaced the smooth Macy's model. A smartly placed pantry, also hand-crafted, filled a once-bare wall.

And, the kitchen. Wow. Double-oven stove and stainless-steel refrigerator, re-stained cabinets and a perfectly sized and placed island, replete with a concrete surface, adding valuable counter space. The cedar countertops? Untouched and blended in just perfectly. The bathrooms? Raised counters with marble countertops. And handsome shadow boxes throughout The Cabin — just "fishing stuff" from the basement DTD told me later. Stuff like my daughter's first life jacket and my dad's old fishing lures.

I called Dianne. "It looks fabulous," I told her. "And it's still The Cabin." She realized that was the ultimate compliment before I added, "So I see you went in the basement?"

There was no way Diane the Decorator could win.

But The Cabin wasn't nearly perfect. It was perfect.

Ten Miles Is Not Very Far

Once you get to The Cabin, it's a pain to go into Milledgeville. Besides being disruptive to cabin activities, 10 miles is a long way.

Nothing against Milledgeville, though. After all, it was the first capital of Georgia, and there are plenty of sites to see. If you like history, there's the Old Governor's Mansion or Memory Hill Cemetery that includes many unmarked graves, slave graves, and graves of patients from the city's mental institution, which also was known as the "Lunatic Asylum." But I never have been a history person.

If you like plants, there's the Lockerly Aboretum. Not my cup of tea. If you like literature, there's Andalusia Museum, once a cotton plantation and farm before becoming the home of author Flannery O'Connor, a novelist who penned, among other pieces, the short story "A Good Man Is Hard To Find." For a heavier dose of culture, there's the Marlo Arts Center. Lighter would be better; never have been much of an arts person.

Milledgeville also has a couple of colleges—Georgia Military College and Georgia College and State University—plus a sizable tech school. Students are everywhere in this town, and there's never a shortage of servers for the many fast-food restaurants.

Restaurants…now that might be a real reason for venturing into Milledgeville. But it takes 10 miles, 10 long miles, to get from The Cabin to Milledgeville. The only real reason to leave The Cabin is when you are hungry or seek a necessity from Lowe's or need bait. And bait is only 4.5 miles away at a four-way stop. So, a trip into Milledgeville is a rarity.

One day I drove the 10 miles to Lowe's, which is across the street from Zaxby's. Yes, Milledgeville has its own Zaxby's. And a couple of Waffle House locations. And an Applebee's — big news when Applebee's came to town. But back to Lowe's. A customer in the checkout line mentioned to the cashier that Zaxby's was relocating. "But just next door to where it is now," the cashier replied.

"Any idea what's going into the old Zaxby's building?" the customer asked. The cashier admitted she was curious but had no idea.

The new Zaxby's might be the best in the Southeast — sparkling new construction, plenty of parking, pretty good wings, and good college-student service. The drive-through window generally has a line of vehicles wrapped around the building as it competes with the Chick-fil-A just down the street where the drive-through line is never short.

But, a few weeks after my Lowe's visit, the longest line of vehicles in the area stretched out onto North Columbia Street for several blocks. And it didn't belong to Zaxby's or Chick-fil-A. The new business at the old Zaxby's location was having its grand opening … and the red light was on. None other than a Krispy Kreme Doughnuts Shop. Milledgeville's own. Mouth-watering, fresh, and hot out of the oven …

So, I have experienced a great awakening. I now know that I should be more culturally enlightened. I need to know more

about Milledgeville's history and plants and literature, so I definitely need to go to town more often. For self-improvement,
of course.

Besides, 10 miles just isn't that far.

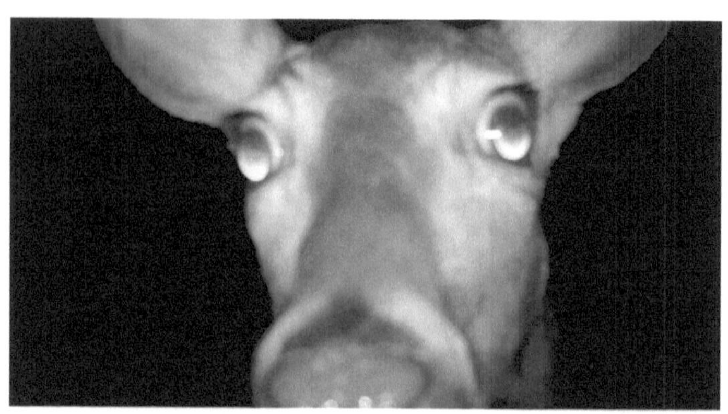

Good To Be Back

It was good to be back at The Cabin. Three weeks without a dose can cause withdrawal symptoms, and my hands were starting to quiver.

"Maybe you should go check on The Cabin," my WW (Wonderful Wife) said out of the blue. She can always tell when it's time, and she's too courteous to say a couple of days without me might be good. I was too courteous to tell her my bag was already packed. Probably why we've been married going on 51 years.

Two hours later I was passing Joe's welding business on Highway 129 about eight miles from The Cabin. Joe had made an iron cover for the lakeside fire pit years ago. The lid weighs a hundred pounds or more but can be raised or lowered with a finger because of the balanced weight system Joe rigged for it. No telling how many racks of ribs have been slow smoked on that fire pit. Couldn't wait for the last eight miles to pass so I could stack some wood in the pit and throw on a couple more racks.

Nothing was really new or different with this arrival at The Cabin, even though our separation had been longer than usual. The field camera was still strapped to the tree where I left it weeks earlier. Trees and leaves littering the driveway were sure signs of a storm, but those are normal in middle Georgia. I couldn't wait to review recent activity on the camera.

I made my way to the creaky screened door on the porch. Nuisance carpenter bees had tried for another hostile takeover. Nothing new about the piles of sawdust left by those nasty tunnel churners. Once found 84 of those destroyers in one plank of the courtyard fence. Removed the plank, flipped it over and let them come out of their tunnels one at a time. Direct hit with bug spray on each one. Used up two cans and not one pest escaped. Thought I was winning the war that day, 84 carpenter bee corpses, but their cousins are constantly getting revenge.

No surprises on the drive-up side porch. Squirrels and chipmunks still think it's their porta potty. They also run there for cover during severe storms, and that's okay. Just wish they would find another bathroom.

The field camera had been set to snap four pictures of any movement around the circle driveway—one picture every two seconds for eight seconds. More than 400 photos were waiting for review. Not surprisingly, the first pictures showed a doe keeping watch over The Cabin. The movement of deer is predictable—early morning and a couple hours after nightfall. Could set your clock by it. They know they are safe near The Cabin.

The fox was not as predictable but always quick. The camera was lucky to get two pictures in the allotted eight seconds and usually could get only one as the fox could scoot by in less than two seconds. Raccoons showed their striped tails forever, and squirrels practically posed for multiple snaps. Stray dogs, we know who you are.

The pest control guy unknowingly hogged a lot of camera time, and workers next door found it easier to use our driveway, which was fine. The Petitt gang hammed it up a couple of times for the camera while cutting, edging, and blowing the grass. Bret and Bradley usually locate the camera while taking care of the property. I cannot show their dad all their shenanigans. The camera doesn't miss much of anything.

The screened porch on the other side of The Cabin, the lake

side, was covered with pollen, the screens seeming to sift that awful stuff into an even finer layer of mess. Hose and mop time for that porch, the rocking chairs and every nick knack neatly placed by my WW. Probably would take half a day to get the screened porch right for the next morning's cup of coffee.

But nothing at The Cabin is a chore. Blowing off the driveway and hosing down the long walkway, no problem. Clearing fallen limbs from a recent storm, no problem. Plugging carpenter bee holes, no problem. Hauling wood for the fire pit, no problem. Putting on two racks of baby back ribs … are you kidding?

Good to be back.

2. Family

Not surprisingly, most of my blogs have been about family. After all, this book was written especially for members of my family. A few updates to family-related blogs: My WW and I had a fun 50th anniversary and are likely to reach 51 — to the same person — before this book is published; doughnuts, especially those of the KK brand, seem to have a place in several blogs; my mother, aka The Warden, is still kickin' at 94 after whipping breast cancer at 93; Aunt Anna is 104 at this writing and still giving stern looks; the population of Eutaw Springs has not changed; Austin is still playing lacrosse and up late at night watching NBA games, Trey is still out-fishing me and not saying any bad words, Neah is as competitive as ever and cheering through high school, Kaisa and Annika are still sugar sweet but likely planning more shenanigans; and, Monica, Dalton and Tyler are enjoying most of their older significant events with Chad, Leslie and Aliina, respectively. If any or none of this makes sense, read on . . .

50 Years to The Same Person

We get the question often. "Just how long have you been married?"

The answer now is 50 years. But my WW (Wonderful Wife) insists on adding, "to the same person."

That's because a friend once told her, "Well, if I add my three marriages together, I probably can get to fifty, too."

So, October 17, 2020, marked the Golden date for us—50 years to the same person, that is. Typically, we did not want any huge fanfare, and it's a good thing because Covid was still making travel risky. No cruise. No long trips. We even decided no flights.

Instead, we opted for one of our favorite trip routines—a drive to the North Carolina mountains with tickets to the Southern Living Idea House in Asheville, a couple of nice bed and breakfast stops, and quick visits with friends along the way. Everyone we encountered seemed genuinely happy for us upon hearing about our 50th, but I was quick to remind them that we still had a day or more to go and we shouldn't take anything for granted. My WW would just smile before reminding everyone that "he's the one who should take nothing for granted."

We reserved a couple of nights at the Biltmore Village Inn, a neat B&B tucked away in an Asheville hillside. I did not recognize what was served for breakfast the next morning. "Just eat it," my WW deadpanned. You can say things like that when you've been married 50 years. "You will like it," she said, knowing very well I wouldn't. It was awful. I remember only the orange juice being good that morning. They had never heard of grits.

After lunch with a good friend, we drove to Charlotte where we checked in at a swanky place called The Duke Mansion. I'd like to say we chose the top floor suite because it was the nicest, but actually it was the only one left when I made the reservation. Certainly a nice place to wake up on your 50th anniversary.

Breakfast the next morning was a white tablecloth affair. I was served asparagus for breakfast for the first time in my life—"Just eat it," my WW deadpanned again, which I did —and I recognized nothing else until the bacon showed up.

While my WW enjoyed her breakfast, she struck up a conversation with our very polite server. The lady had been at The Duke Mansion for many years which prompted my WW to tell her that it was our 50th anniversary. "Actually, we have eleven hours to go, and we shouldn't take anything for granted," I injected. Joan just smiled, "and I'm thinking about trading him in for a newer model."

The server enjoyed her time with us and brought us a complimentary dessert that I didn't recognize but ate nonetheless. The entire breakfast included a variety of piped-in music. We could not have asked for a more appropriate tune as we sipped our last coffee to "Going to the chapel and we're going to get married…". True. Then, as we left the room, unbelievably, Randy Travis serenaded us with, "I'm going to love you forever and ever and ever…".

I guess the blog could and maybe should end with Randy Travis. But we weren't quite to 50 years yet. We agreed our last stop should be in South Carolina to see my 93-year-old mother. Because of Covid, we met her outside where my sister had set up chairs for us.

"You know you're the first in the family to celebrate 50 years," my mother said.

"To the same person, too," my WW said.

"We've still got a couple hours so we shouldn't take anything for granted," I said. We all had a good laugh.

We made it to 50 on the ride home … 50 years to the same person … best ride of my life.

The Doughnut Hole

My Dad's Dad was a gentle soul. We called him Paw.

Paw was crusty and tough as nails but truly gentle. Especially when it came to his grandchildren. Years of hard work at Charleston's Navy Yard scarred him in hardened hands and salty language, but we never heard those bad words from Paw's mouth.

We loved when Paw and Mammy would come for a visit. Those visits initially were from Charleston and in later years from Florida. While we were obliged to be polite about it, we weren't necessarily interested in seeing Mammy and all her furs and rings and other jewelry. But it was a different feeling for Paw and his plaid flannel shirts and scuffed shoes.

"Now remember to save me the hole from your doughnut," he would say as we each took a Krispy Kreme. It took several years for us to realize that it was impossible to save the hole for Paw. We would carefully eat from the outer edge to the center and then take a thin ring to him. "Not yet," he would say. "I think you need to eat a little bit more, but just a little bit … but save me the hole." Of course, that next bit, or the next, always meant the ring would be broken and the hole would disappear. "Oh no, maybe next time." And then Paw would smile. Always a smile.

Paw also convinced us that our yard on Margrave Road had buried treasures in a lot of places. All we had to do was find them. And most of the time the treasures could be found near the doodlebug mounds where he would nudge us. Remarkably, he was always right.

The treasures often were pennies, nickels, or dimes, sometimes quarters, and the coins always were found inside small match boxes that were buried just below the surface of the ground. Match boxes, ironically, that were just like the ones in Paw's shirt pocket. We thought we were rich some days after those treasure hunts under the front-yard Chinaberry tree where Paw always met us after meals. We had no idea how rich those treasures were.

We loved Paw. We were too young to understand why his hardened hands would sometimes shake during his later years. And he seemed to get emotional at times while telling us stories about when he was a little boy. And when it was time to tell us goodbye after visiting, well, he just couldn't. In his final couple of years, he would leave the house first, get in the car and just wait with tears streaming. He never wanted us to see him cry.

"Paw has a hard time saying goodbye," my mother would

say. We learned later that Paw feared it might be the last time he would see us. And then that visit came.

The drive to Florida for Paw's funeral was long and quiet. My Dad was especially quiet, but he held his emotions inside. He never wanted us to see him cry. I'm not sure he ever got over Paw's death. He never talked about it.

My Dad's hands were hardened, too, from hard work. And he loved telling my young children stories about when he was a little boy. And he was always trying to get them to save that hole in the doughnut. Crusty and tough as nails, but another gentle soul.

His grandchildren called him Paw Paw.

Grandmother's Memory

Grandmother had but one request before leaving Columbia for an assisted living facility in Atlanta.

She wanted to visit her mother's grave.

Of course, we will, I told her, knowing well that the visit most likely would be her last to the cemetery in the Cedar Creek community. And it was.

"Before we go, I need you to get the box out of the trunk of my car," she said. "We'll need to take it to the cemetery with us."

I knew not to ask a lot of questions. Grandmother, my

WW's mother whose memory was being infected with dementia, was always direct with her requests. Stubborn might be a better word. Or, demanding. But this request certainly was reasonable, one that my WW definitely wanted to please, and it did not hinder our plan for getting her to Atlanta—something she had strongly resisted when thinking straight.

But Grandmother no longer was thinking straight often enough to be on her own. My WW had made arrangements for the disposition of her house on Betsy Drive and visited a dozen assisted living sites near us in Roswell before settling on the most suitable. Grandmother knew nothing of the plan to move her until we sat alone in her small living room where curtains always were pinned back with clothespins so she could snoop on neighbors. Her biggest fear was being put in a "damn nursing home" and I promised her we would never do that. I simply told her it was time she lived with us a while.

Grandmother relented in her own way, never agreeing. She picked up the phone and called her neighbor Ann. "I guess I'm going to one of those places called assisted living," she said. "I love you. Bye." And that's when she asked if I would take her to her mother's grave before we left for Atlanta.

The ride to the Cedar Creek cemetery from Betsy Drive was about 45 minutes. Along the way, Grandmother told me again she did not want to go to a nursing home. I assured her we would not let that happen. "Did you get that box out of the trunk of my car?" she asked. "We're going to need it at the cemetery." I told her I had the box and asked her what was in it. "We're going to decorate the cemetery," she said. "Mother would like that."

I certainly was not going to press the point, but decorate the cemetery? I turned into Cedar Creek Methodist Church, established 1743, and pulled up to the cemetery gate behind the church. We walked to the Rabon family plot that was well defined by a short brick wall and a cyclone fence behind it. "We need to decorate that fence," Grandmother declared as though she had planned this project for some time. "Now, go get that box out of the car."

Being the trusted son-in-law, I did as I was told. I peeked inside the box before taking it from the car and saw an assortment of plastic flowers, strings of tinsel, what looked to be colorful Hawaiian leis, and a few other really tacky items. Surely, we weren't going to … but we did. We spent the next 45 minutes attaching all those items to the fence, providing an incredibly gaudy backdrop. Right when I started to think we could be arrested for this, I turned to Grandmother.

"Isn't it beautiful?" she asked.

There was only one answer. "Yes, Grandmother. Indeed, it is beautiful."

We then hurried to the car and drove off before the sheriff could arrive. Grandmother asked why I was laughing. "It's nothing, Grandmother, really … nothing."

The ride back, like this entire experience, was memorable. While she did not remember being at the cemetery, she could vividly recall details from her childhood as we rode through areas from her past. "My friends and I used to play in that backyard," she remembered, pointing to a dilapidated house. "We would hang clothes on the clothesline." She was sure of it. And I thought to myself, that was probably 80 years ago.

Grandmother lived with us several weeks in Roswell while my WW finalized arrangements for a move to the assisted living facility just down the road from us. My WW, as only she can do, insisted on a room near the front of the facility with a window so her mother could watch people come and go. She even had the clothespins necessary to hold the curtains back—just like Betsy Drive. "You know she's very nosy," my WW understated. Furniture from Betsy Drive also made the assisted living suite more like home.

But Grandmother knew nothing of her reserved room at the assisted living facility. And every time we broached the subject of assisted living her response was the same. "Sounds like a nursing home," she insisted. But she also insisted on having her hair appointments—forever an important part of her life. So, my ingenious WW made the next hair appointment … at the assisted living beauty parlor. The day of the appointment, everybody was aware of our plan except Grandmother, who gazed at the interior of the nice facility as we walked her through the front doors and to the beauty parlor without a word.

"Everybody here is so nice," Grandmother acknowledged as she left the parlor after having her hair done. She then paused. "This is so nice. Is it one of those places you call assisted living?" Risking the entire scheme, I encouraged her to "come along, we just don't have the time to … " But she stopped. "Do you think we could look around?" Which we did, finishing our tour at her suite where she remarked, "That even looks like some of my old furniture."

And it became her last home.

A couple weeks later, while taking a walk around the grounds, we stopped to get a view of the assisted living facility from atop a hill where she looked out with a smile.

"Isn't it beautiful?" she asked.

There was only one answer. "Yes, Grandmother. Indeed, it is beautiful."

Touching Some Roots

Eutaw Springs, S.C., is a suburb, so to speak, of Eutawville which is a suburb, so to speak, of Holly Hill. When the census-sanctioned population of Holly Hill is 1,281 and the population of Eutawville is 344, and you are Eutaw Springs, really, there can't be much to you.

Except for the memories.

And the memories returned as we knocked off the miles while traveling through Augusta, then Aiken, then Columbia, and then almost to Orangeburg before exiting I-26 in search of the old route I often took to Eutaw Springs and Lake Marion as a youngster.

My Aunt Lackie had lived 89 years, reared three children the right way, earned a reputation for honesty and integrity, and added immeasurably to three communities. She lived in Eutaw Springs, worked in Eutawville and worshipped in Holly Hill. No finer lady has ever graced this earth, so our trip back for the celebration of her life included some sadness but mostly memories that are relived with smiles and laughter.

Such memories of this three-town stretch many times involve my cousins—Babs, Gail, and Jamie—when we were tots and then pre-teens. The most stress we knew back then came during our Monopoly games. Life was simple because life was still ahead of us. And all three of these lives today and their families are wonderful examples for others after all these years.

My parents eventually had property on Lake Marion, and it was a great getaway back in the sixties for my teenage fishing buddies and me. Four of us would cram into a VW bug and hit the road for an overnighter at Eutaw Springs. Sleeping quarters the first few trips were on the floor in a one-room shack with a rough bathroom off the back—good enough for guys until my Dad could add on and eventually turn it into a more comfortable house. The one-room shack was more fun.

Back then, trips to Eutaw Springs were never complete without at least one meal at Danny Bell's Restaurant. We didn't need menus. Fried catfish. Every time for everybody. Danny Bell would sometimes serve us personally and tell us how the crappie and bream were biting. If anybody knew, it was Danny Bell. He was sort of a Eutaw Springs hero.

Blount's Store was across the street from the restaurant. Mrs. Blount sold us our bait and usually had her own scoop on whether the fish were biting—and which ones. I sometimes suspected Mrs. Blount would tell us the crappie were active because minnows cost us more than worms, which was to her cash register's advantage. Usually, we could only afford the worms anyway.

Blount's Store is no longer there, but Danny Bell's Restaurant is, and signs still advertise the popular fried catfish. Just down the road a neat official green sign now proclaims Highway 6 to be "Danny Bell Highway." Rightly so.

Not much else has changed, and I think Aunt Lackie would like it that way. She and Uncle Jimmy moved into the renovated and enlarged house that was once the one-room shack and enjoyed comfortable waterfront life there for many years. The evening before her funeral, Aunt Lackie's neighbors made sure food at her house was aplenty for visiting family and friends. While we were there, Cousin Jamie, for my sake, stepped off the part of the house that was once the one-room shack. It made sense, but I never would have figured it out on my own.

Jamie also mentioned that he found my dad's old fishing boat and locked it up inside a fence in Eutawville in case I ever wanted it. My WW and I made time to see the boat the following day; still had a couple of the same seats and what looked to be the same gas tank. After about 65 years, the boat needs some cleaning up and repairs, but it no longer needs an owner.

The service the next day in Holly Hill was quite a tribute to Aunt Lackie. Most times when you are 89, a lot of your friends and family have already departed earth, and attendance at your funeral could be sparse at best. Not this time. Half of Holly Hill, Eutawville, and Eutaw Springs crowded into the pews of the First Baptist Church of Holly Hill to pay their respects, and it took three ministers to adequately share some of the highlights of her life.

The service was considered a celebration of life rather than a funeral. For me, however, these occasions are sad. I especially hurt for my three favorite cousins. Babs, Gail, and Jamie are strong in their faith, though, and time will help. Their parents certainly taught them well.

After the cemetery service just behind the church, we hugged family and friends and said our goodbyes to my cousins. A long ride back to Georgia awaited us, but not before one more out-of-the-way trip down Danny Bell Highway.

It took all of about 10 minutes from Holly Hill to Eutawville to that gnat of a suburb called Eutaw Springs. Not much to it.

Except for the memories.

91 And Still Kicking Hard

She's been called Mama, Nene, Annette, Granny, GG... and, perhaps most accurately, The Warden.

This lady who has never really looked out for herself seems always to be looking out for everybody else. Especially family, which includes her eight sisters and one brother—of whom only three still survive. But Mama Huguley is still kicking... and kicking hard. She intentionally has slowed down some, mostly so she can watch tennis and golf on TV, but her mind has not skipped a beat.

As Mama, she kept an eagle eye on her brood of five as they were growing up. Once marched into the principal's office at Eau Claire High School to take sides with one of her children in a dispute with a sassy teacher. The principal got the point. At the end of the school year, the teacher got the boot. When that little episode was over, Mama didn't mention it again. No need to talk it up or brag or spread the word. Why bother; just get on with life.

As Mama, she was firm—perhaps putting it lightly. Her children didn't necessarily appreciate her bluntness as teenagers, but they always understood the difference between right and wrong. It was kinda like, "Let me set you straight on something…" and then came the lesson. The unadulterated truth. The gospel. Not surprising that her five kids stayed on the straight and narrow. Still do.

As Nene, the name she was called by her Greek sisters, she excelled in school, studied nursing, and even won a silver cup as a ping pong champion. She, her brother and seven sisters survived a devastating tornado in 1938 that wiped out the family grocery store on Rutledge Avenue in Charleston, S.C. Her parents, the first Greek immigrants to be married in Charleston—as evidenced by "No. 1" on their marriage license—didn't flinch. Rousso's Grocery was rebuilt replete with living quarters above for the large family.

As Nene, she must have inherited her grit from her dad, called Pappoo by the huge extended family. Once a week, Pappoo would take his small boat out into the Atlantic Ocean, alone, to fish—at age 81. Then he would go back to Rutledge Avenue, swig his daily toddy, and take his nap.

As Annette, in her late teens she ran around with Johnny Huguley, who lived a block away on Race Street. They married, thought it would be clever to name their boys Tom, Dick and Harry, which they did, although they had Susie and Debbie before finally getting Harry.

As Annette, she held the family together as my dad worked hard and long to provide for the family of seven. No complaints from her when they moved from Charleston to Florida, back to Charleston, then to Columbia for more moves from Mountain Drive to Lincoln Street to Park Street to Highlawn Avenue (later named Margrave Road) and then to Ridgeway. Two bedrooms, one bathroom, family of seven … no complaints. Cramped but happy times — youth baseball and softball and basketball teams, church on Sundays, rides back to Charleston, trips to the beach, ice cream cones on the weekends and a big Christmas every year. We certainly had everything we needed and didn't know what we didn't have.

As Granny, she adores her grandchildren. As GG, she adores her great grandchildren. She regularly rotates family pictures on her den shelves, careful to treat everybody the same. It would not be like her to have a favorite. She will tell you that each one is her favorite. She loves her own suite at daughter Debbie's home in Blythewood, and she still drives — sometimes long distances. Debbie and hubby Joe, by the way, have free passes to Heaven for eliminating questions — 25 years ago — about our mother's future before they arose for the family.

And, The Warden? Well, some friends of her children stuck that label on her many years ago. Her disciplinarian nature is the source. In earlier years she could be fairly direct, let's say, so there could be no mistaking her message. Like, don't mess with my kids. Or, do as I say do, not as I do. Or, when I say curfew is 11 o'clock, I mean 11 o'clock. Plain and simple. I think my mother sorta likes being called The Warden.

So, on January 13, 2018, The Warden celebrated her 91st birthday. During a telephone call, she told me she feels pretty good for someone who's beginning to get old. She asked about her grandchildren and great grandchildren—always deflecting attention away from herself. Then she told me she would be making another drive from Blythewood to Charleston soon to take her 99-year-old sister to a doctor's appointment. There would not be even an attempt to talk her out of it.

After all, she said, she is much younger than her sister. And, at 91 she's still kicking hard.

Aunt Anna at 100

For a hundred years, everybody has loved Aunt Anna.

Just not all the time.

The oldest of eight sisters, she has outlasted all but two. Only her brother was born before her, and Costa passed away years ago. Can you imagine being Costa with eight Greek sisters in the house, competing for bathroom use or looking for quiet time?

But this isn't about Costa, a dear uncle who invented patience. It's about Aunt Anna, the first of eight Rousso girls who grew up mostly on Rutledge Avenue in Charleston before marrying Jimmy Friend and having two children, Pee Wee and El-len. Pee Wee was a boyhood hero of mine because he was a darn good baseball player, "damn good" if you ask Aunt Anna. Ellen was smart and sweet; probably inherited the intelligence from her mom but not the sweetness. As cousins were known to say, certainly not within earshot of their aunt, "Aunt Anna can be mean." Actually, she didn't really care what you said.

But I never considered Aunt Anna to be mean. Even when we would visit her in her pristine house as a youngster. My mother would warn us, "Don't touch a thing when you go in-side," and we knew to obey. Aunt Anna invented the word pris-tine right after the word immaculate. I once commented how nice a trinket looked; "Don't touch it," she barked with a frown. And I didn't dare.

If you were brave enough to touch one of her hundreds of trinkets, or even if you moved too close to one, you could risk admonishment that you'd never forget. And, that look, that stern look. My mother would always tell us, "Just sit there on the couch and don't move."

But, again, I never considered Aunt Anna to be mean. Ev-ery time she worked me over with that frown and stern look, I kept looking at her until I saw the slight smile. That was the giveaway.

She has outlived Jimmy Friend, two children, second hus-band Bill Utsey, as well as five sisters, her brother, and plenty of nieces and nephews. She has never been on an elevator, proba-bly doesn't trust them, and has lived long enough for her doctor to come to her house rather than the other way around. She likely gave him an ultimatum. During the most recent hurricanes to come through Charleston, she stayed put. Asking her to leave was a waste of breath; insisting she leave would get you a death threat. And her yard today, even after hurricane battering, is like her house of trinkets 80 years ago. Spotless. You don't want to be her gardener.

But beneath that stern look, if you look closely...really, that hint of a slight smile. Aunt Anna's frown, most times anyway, was followed by that smile that she tried hard to keep out of sight. She had a reputation to live up to and she was good at it. Still is.

At her 100th birthday celebration, which she did not want to have, everybody showed up. Nobody touched a trinket, but everybody showed up.

For a hundred years, everybody has loved Aunt Anna.

A Barbie for Gram

My WW is called Gram by our grandchildren.

Anybody who knows Gram also knows you'd better not mess with her kids or grandkids. Anything less than complimentary will get you deep in the doghouse of this five-foot grandmother.

Gram also has house rules for the grandchildren: 1) No grandchild will ever get in trouble while at Gram and Grandad's house; 2) You do not have to clean your plate; 3) Toys from the toy closet are allowed anywhere in the house; and, 4) Any grandchild is allowed to visit the pantry anytime.

You get the idea.

Gram's rules are much more reasonable than Grandad's one rule: at least one piece of chocolate every visit — at least one.

Gram also believes in playing with the grandkids when they visit. Everything else is put on hold. This is especially true when Kaisa and Annika visit. K is five, Anka three and they love to play with Gram whether it's an imaginary safari through the house or — their favorite — playing with their Barbie dolls.

Gram had a big surprise for them last visit. She had purchased a large Barbie house replete with rooftop swimming pool, three floors and all things Barbie. It was set up and ready to go when they arrived. The biggest surprise, however, was yet to come.

Gram also had purchased her own Barbie doll, Nurse Barbie. And that opened a whole new world of imagination. Nurse Barbie assumed two little nursing assistants who began taking care of Gram, the other Barbies and … Grandad, who was summoned from his recliner to be a patient. After being subjected to blood pressure checks, ear and nose checks, knee reflex hammers, injections, and numerous temp checks, he was declared healthy but told to cut down on the chocolate.

K and Anka had a ton of fun with Gram and the Barbie house, and their excitement was obvious. But, most of all, they just could not believe that Gram had her own Barbie. Such a cool Gram.

So, how many grandmothers aged 60-something have their own Barbie? This one was about to celebrate a birthday, making her 60-something-plus-one. And, like many grandmothers, Gram is not easy to buy for on any such occasion.

Well, March 11 came with the usual morning birthday coffee and opening of cards and gifts. Gram was her usual chatty self for 8 o'clock in the morning. She could guess most of her gifts before opening them—the small hand vacuum she requested for when the grandgirls snack at their Princess table, a gift card for car washes, the smallest Totes umbrella ever made. But there was one mystery gift.

The final gift was tucked away in a medium sized birthday bag and saved for last. Gram is pretty good at guessing gifts, but this one stumped even her. Nothing left to do but dive into that bag of tissue paper. No doubt, Gram loved the surprise and could not wait to show it and share it with Kaisa and Annika.

This 60-something-plus-one grandmother is now the proud owner of her own bright pink Barbie sports car—a convertible no less. Just what Gram—and the grandgirls—needed.

After all, Gram already has her own Barbie.

A Fishing Boat Named

All boats should have a name.

You never want to say, "Let's go fishing in THE BOAT." The boat needs a name—sometimes odd but usually meaningful.

My Dad, a skilled craftsman, actually built his first boat. He set up shop on the open carport on Margrave Road. As he had the time and money, he would piddle with it. Wooden, carefully measured, every cut precise. It was a 12-foot boat for pond use only. Sturdy, and the good part: it actually would float. I also learned some bad words during that project on the carport, but that's off the subject.

"Our boat needs a name," he said. My Dad always used "our" when talking about his possessions. He thought everything he had should be shared, especially with his children. Nothing ever belonged to just him.

"We need to think about a name," he said. He always wanted to think for a while before making a profound decision. "What about Todiha?" he blurted as though he already had thought long and hard about it. Pronounced tah-dee-hay…

"What? What in the world is Todiha?"

"You know… Tom, Dick and Harry… the first two letters of…"

So, the name of that gray, wooden boat forever would be ToDiHa, named after his three boys. As in, "You want to go fishing in the ToDiHa?"

The ToDiHa had a few excursions before expiring. Maybe it sank or was sold or became firewood, but its name has remained in the family and many times has come up at family gatherings. A story and name worth remembering.

Fast forward about 55 years to 2015 and a gray, aluminum 16-foot Polar Craft, comfortably docked near The Cabin. Definitely not constructed in an open carport, but desperately in need of a name. MoDaTy, after our three children—Monica, Dalton and Tyler—just did not have the right ring to it; maybe even a hint of hip hop. No way. But, with five grandchildren back then and a sixth on the way, maybe…

Let's see, from oldest to youngest, there was Hunter, Austin, Trey, Neah and Kaisa with number six to be born in 2015. Playing scramble the first letters of the five names, amazingly…T-H-A-N-K. Which meant if we could get an "S" with grandchild number six, what better name for our fishing boat than "THANKS"—named in appreciation of our grandchildren? Only one problem: we needed an "S". Would the name of grandchild number six possibly, miraculously, start with an "S"?

Since this plan was in my warped mind only, I wondered if dropping very discreet hints might steer the name game in the direction of an "S". So, minding someone else's business, I offered, "Since you know you're having a girl, I really like the name Samantha." Moans and groans could be heard around the block. I thought of Sharon and Sara and Sylvia and…but I knew, really, it was none of my business. I would just have to take my chances.

Well, Annika was born in February of 2015, and my name game was done.

But all boats should have a name. Maybe odd but meaningful.

THANKA is perfect for our boat.

The Heart of a Kid

It's not unusual to talk sports with grandson Austin, although I did have to brush up on lacrosse terminology and strategy and rules the past four years. That's because Austin was generally considered one of the two best high school lacrosse players in Louisiana his senior year. But this isn't about ability or bragging about a grandson.

This is about the kind heart of a kid.

The question was simple: Austin wanted to know my thoughts about the best pro basketball player ever to play the game. Wilt Chamberlain came to mind along with Bill Russell, but those two were from an era too far gone for Austin to relate. "What about Michael Jordan and Larry Bird?" he asked. "Which one of those was better?" I could have offered a couple of smart aleck answers … like … it depends on what city you were from, Chicago or Boston, or … it depends on whether you were a Bulls fan or a Celtics fan. But I didn't because it seemed like Austin was seriously curious about how yesteryear's professional players might rank with today's players.

So, my answer was, "Jordan probably was the best, but Bird was definitely my favorite." Then I sent him a highlight video of Bird, which he loved.

It's common for Austin to be awake around midnight during the NBA season, watching west coast games. He loves basketball as much as lacrosse. But this isn't about basketball either. When Austin's senior season of high school lacrosse was ready to tip off—or whatever you do to start a lacrosse game—he was captain of his team and ready for a banner year after setting multiple school records as an underclassman. Opponents knew their best hope was to triple team him, a strategy that often was not successful. A stack of letters from college lacrosse coaches was evidence enough of Austin's skills.

The first game of his senior season, however, never really started for him. Before any contact at all, he dropped to his knees in pain and could barely breathe. Making it worse, he did not know why. He was rushed to the hospital where doctors determined he had suffered a spontaneous pneumothorax—the sudden onset of a collapsed lung without any apparent cause.

No physical contact. No pre-game jitters. No nothing. It just happened at this particular time in his life. Following two agonizing weeks in the hospital, surgery was necessary. After lots of agony for him and even more agonizing by his mother, his lung finally was able to maintain full inflation on its own.

While Austin's lung proved to be really stubborn, there was nothing wrong with his heart. Two weeks after leaving the hospital, he was back on the lacrosse field. He finished his senior season, won numerous awards, and was named to the All-State lacrosse team despite missing part of the year. The untimely challenge with his collapsed lung obviously did not keep him down long.

But this really isn't about a lung either. It's about the kind heart of a thoughtful kid.

Austin's motive behind the Larry Bird-Michael Jordan conversations was sneaky. He knew his grandparents were coming to Louisiana for a Christmas visit. As it turned out, our eight-hour drive was well worth it. He had saved his money from part-time work to order a special (and expensive) gift for Grandad.

The official, NBA certified Larry Bird game jersey — replete with the famous number "33" and even more famous name "Bird" — now hangs in my home office. I will treasure the jersey of my favorite basketball player … but not nearly as much as my favorite lacrosse player.

Endorsement for RDH III

Chip off the old block? Hardly. Even though he has the same name.

Trey generally excels at whatever he chooses to do. In his young life it was fishing and hunting. Whether he's with friend Mikey or his namesake Dad or Grandad, he seemed to have a nose for finding the fish — or deer.

Trey learned to aim straight at an early age with a BB and pellet rifle. He and the rifle were the same height. The early training paid off after a couple years with his first eight-point buck. He also trained early with a bow and arrow made with his own hands — with a little help from his Grandad. He now helps to educate his Grandad on things like the best models of hunting rifles and the gear ratios on baitcasting reels. He even has made his own lures for fly fishing.

If this is bragging about a grandson, so be it.

Trey once was pond fishing with a friend. Might have been one of those times they were fishing a pond they weren't supposed to be fishing. Anyway, this excursion was unplanned, so he did not have his tackle box, only a borrowed pole with limited line, one bream hook and no bait. For the uneducated, a bream hook is very small. Two fancy-pants guys were fishing the same pond — probably with permission, of all things — and tossed a used and battered plastic worm toward Trey and his friend. "Why don't you try that?" they laughed.

Trey, as always, was polite. "Okay, thanks." He then divided the worm with his friend, something only a good guy would do. Trey took his small piece of plastic worm, embedded the bream hook, and tied it to his limited piece of fishing line. Maybe you can guess the rest of this fish tale, which happens to be true. Trey surveyed the pond for just the right spot, tossed the concocted lure near some weeds in the water and, bingo! Dragged in a nice largemouth bass. Didn't want to rub it in too badly, but while inspecting his trophy he held it just high enough for the two fancy-pants guys to get a glimpse.

Another true tale: At age six, during a trip to The Cabin, Trey and his Grandad decided to do some bream fishing. "How many crickets do you think we should get, twenty-five or fifty?" I asked him. Trey decided on one hundred crickets, launched the jon boat and headed to one of our secret honey holes. When the sun started going down, we motored back to

The Cabin with 82 bream and zero crickets. He just couldn't stop fishing until every cricket was gone.

Trey was invited to go to south Florida for some fishing with a friend. Wasn't long before the pictures started arriving. Then a text with a picture: "Added a new species today … a cichlid." Trey keeps track of the different species of fish he has caught since he first started fishing. The cichlid upped the number to 33. The next day, a video arrived of Trey pulling in a hammerhead shark. Not surprisingly, he played the shark perfectly to the boat. "Caught it on light tackle and 20-pound test line," he texted. Experienced fishermen understand the difficulty of such a challenge. Trey was 15 years old

Trey also has learned to maneuver in today's technology-dominated, social media world. He recently fished in an on-line fishing tournament. Pay a small fee, get a code, and register any fish caught by submitting a picture of the fish next to an approved measuring device. It involves an honor system, which is right up Trey's alley. Anything dishonest just isn't in his DNA. Didn't win the tournament but had fun and gained some experience.

Because he caught plenty of good-sized fish, pictures of his catches sometimes appeared on social media. That led to contacts with outdoors marketers and fishing equipment manufacturers. He has been asked to wear certain logo shirts and use certain fishing equipment—such as particular name-brand weights for his fishing line. Trey is not apt to be endorsing products anytime soon, but marketers might be wise to keep him in their sights.

I'd endorse this guy … this grandson … any day.

The Real Winners

Neah's team really didn't have much hope of winning...but don't dare tell 12-year-olds anything like that. Her basketball team had only six players. The other team had plenty of substitutes and used a full court press the whole game. Yes, the opponents were bigger and faster. But they were about to be thrown into a hornet's nest, and they didn't know what they were in for.

The game was played at a dot on the Georgia map called Ball Ground. More specifically, at the City Gym. The Ball Ground City Gym was probably built a thousand years ago. Some parents watching the game attended school nearby and played in the same gym. After all these years, the basketball floor is perfect and the bleachers, totally wooden, are as solid as one large slab of granite. Aluminum, as in material used for bleachers in most modern gyms today, had not been invented when Ball Ground City Gym was constructed. But Ball Ground the town is booming. It has earned its own exit off I-575 and is only 19 miles from the Woodstock exit. I know the distance because I had to get there in record time after spending a couple of hours with two other granddaughters in Roswell. Kaisa and Annika were pumped about Gram and Grandad coming at 5 o'clock to babysit, and we were equally excited. After a large pizza—half cheese and half pepperoni as requested by K and A via video text earlier in the day—it was wild playtime in the basement followed by the dreaded bedtime. In between was a secret piece of chocolate, but "we can't tell my mom and dad" per Kaisa.

My WW volunteered to put the two girls down and encouraged me not to be late for Neah's game. That's when I realized you cannot get to Ball Ground from Roswell. At least not in one hour on a Friday evening. So, I left a little early after a couple of hugs and kisses. With huge thanks to GPS, I made it to Ball Ground with six minutes to spare, even after not trusting GPS and making three wrong turns.

Neah's team wore white uniforms, but they might as well have been yellow and black swarming bees. Not known for a potent offense, the white team came out with a sticky, shifty, stinging defense that smothered the team in black. It was 3-0 late in the first quarter, and the favored black jerseys had the noticeable zero. They were stunned. Truth be told, everybody was stunned. Except maybe the girls in white.

All that first-quarter energy took a bit of zip out of Neah's team in the second period, but only a bit. The good girls—I mean, the white jerseys—trailed by only a couple of points at halftime. And after the halftime rest, Neah and her mates were nagging wasps again. They allowed only one basket in the third quarter while Neah kept her team in the game with a huge basket of her own. Entering the final period, palms were sweaty, and perspiration was dripping—and that was from the stressed-out parents and spectators.

The team in black endured another period of suffocating defense as the white jerseys refused to give up in the final quarter. The relentless scrambling for the ball created absolute chaos for the girls in black, but they managed to survive. "Glad that's over," one black jersey mumbled after the game. Her next thought surely was, "Hope we don't have to play them again."

Grandparents are proud of their grandchildren, win or lose. Sometimes they are prouder when they lose than when they win. And they are really proud when they get to have a picture taken after the game with the toughest competitor on the floor.

A few minutes before the picture, red-faced and drained

with fatigue, Neah and her teammates offered handshakes and congrats to the scoreboard winners.

The other winners, the real winners, wore the white jerseys that night in Ball Ground.

Bless Their Sweetened Hearts

Grandchildren love healthy snacks like doughnuts, Little Debbie cakes, chewing gum, and maybe some Neccos (pure sugar wafers). With all that sugar, no wonder Kaisa and Annika are sweet. Most of the time.

The sugary stuff is plentiful at Grandad and Gram's house despite pleas from their parents. Pleas eventually turn into parental declarations, and we try to cooperate. Really.

"Okay, they can have chocolate, but we'll pick them up about four hours after the last piece," their Dad declared. "We need time for all that sugar to get through their system. Better still, maybe eight hours."

We grandparents fail to see the point although we once witnessed a meltdown by Annika after having a Sprite at McDonald's. The girl was swinging from the Golden Arches in five minutes. "See," said sister Kaisa, "It's the Sprite."

But these two grandgirls are mostly sweet even without the sugar. Meaning most of the time.

We tried hard to come up with a reason, more like an excuse, for their actions one day in their own home. Curiosity must have gotten the best of them that day. They share a bathroom in their home and have a double vanity.

They were just curious. What would happen if they turned on the water in both bathroom sinks and put the stoppers in—and left the stoppers in? And left the water running while they went to play.

Well, a lot happens and nothing very good. Especially when the double sinks on the upper level of their three-story home overflow—for a long time. Of course, water always flows to the lowest point, in this case to the bottom floor. And it can damage a lot in between including carpet, hardwood floors, ceilings, walls, and a lot of other expensive things.

As grandparents, we tried hard to help them out: they didn't know any better; a learning experience; just curious; maybe someone broke into your house; do you have a dog?

Really, though, these are two sweet grandgirls. Really. But there is one other … situation.

They both love visiting The Cabin with their parents. Gram and Grandad were going to be on vacation so Kaisa and Annika would have to survive this particular lake trip with only their parents. It was a good week of hot-weather swimming, playing in the basement and resting on the long, screened porch. The porch is a favorite lakeside spot with rocking chairs and several foot stools. And the irrigation control box.

Innocently enough, curiosity got the best of Kaisa and Annika again. The door of the control box slipped open—all by itself—and the arrow on the dial looked like it was made to spin. After all, it looked just like those arrows that spin on their board games. Chutes and Ladders comes to mind. And those small foot stools fit a couple of small fannies just perfectly. No telling how many times they took turns spinning the arrow and pushing buttons.

And that freshly planted sod in the courtyard on the other side of The Cabin, the specialty sod that was delivered from South Georgia, the sod that needed watering twice daily, the sod that was doing so very well a week earlier. Well, that sod …

Kaisa, Annika, and their parents left The Cabin after a week, oblivious to any issue with the courtyard sod. Property manager Jason came a few days later before making the call to us. "The sod was healthy ten days ago," he said. "Now it's fried. Dead."

What could have happened? "Well," Jason hesitated. "It won't survive without water."

Jason had checked the irrigation control box. The cover was still open with two small stools pulled up to it.

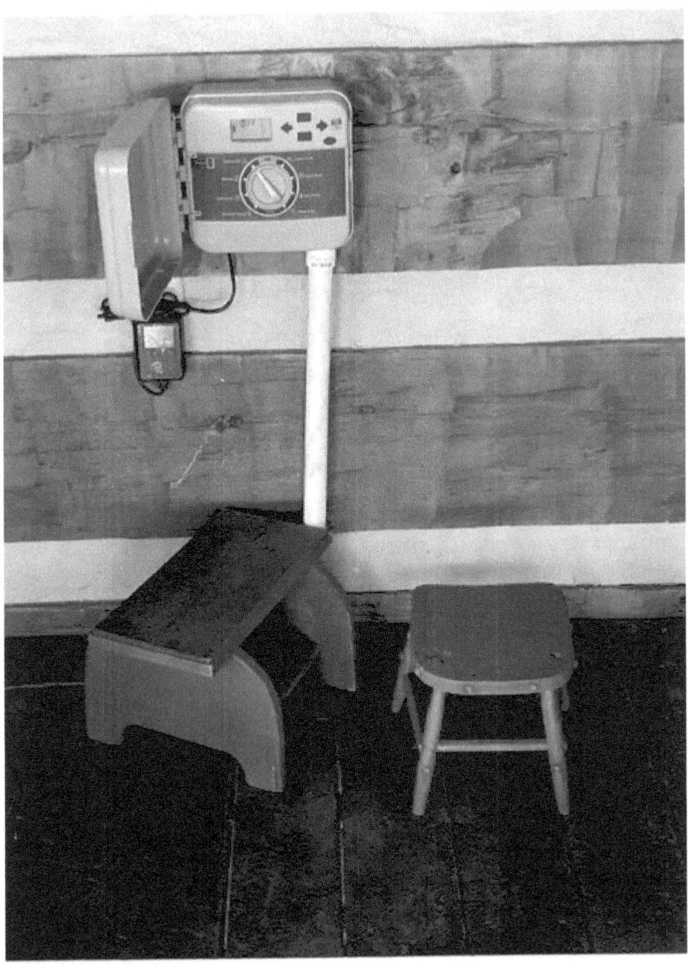

"When can you get back to South Georgia for some more of that special sod? And, let's pick up a lock for that control box," I told Jason.

And what about sweet Kaisa and Annika? Well, it wasn't really their fault. They were just curious and, besides, there was no lock on the box. Maybe neighbor Bill turned off the control box. Who knows what really happened? Bless their sweetened hearts.

Maybe we'll tell them and their parents about it one day. Or maybe they will read about it in a blog.

We Needed A Miracle

Do you believe in miracles? Let me tell you about one.

Dr. Williams came in to talk to my WW and me. It was late in the evening at Crawford Long Hospital in Atlanta in 1987. He wanted to brief us on the surgery he would perform on our younger son the next morning. Tyler was expected to survive the open-heart surgery, but prospects for a healthy life beyond that were bleak at best.

With the uncertainty of heart surgery on a six-year-old and likely valve replacement, Dr. Williams explained, the future would include blood thinners for life, on-going appointments with specialists, additional surgeries, and much reduced activities—including sports—as Tyler matured. We should be prepared for a significant life change for Tyler and us.

A few weeks prior, as part of relocating to Atlanta, we were changing doctors and transferring records from S.C. when we met Dr. Rastegar, a pediatric cardiologist who would perform a simple heart murmur check on Tyler with his stethoscope. Our doctor back in S.C. had maintained since Tyler's birth that the murmur and a tiny hole were normal and would disappear with his growth. Dr. Rastagar's stethoscope told him something entirely different after just one examination. When he asked my WW and me to step into a conference room, we had palpitations of our own.

Dr. Rastegar was quickly to the point. Tyler's heart issue was much more than a murmur and small hole that usually closes on its own with time. Tyler was going to need heart surgery and there was not a lot of time to waste. With help from my new newspaper colleagues, we identified the top pediatric cardiologist surgeon in the region.

Dr. Williams' office reviewed Tyler's test results and records and agreed to add him as a patient. But there was just one nerve-wracking dilemma: the wait list for Dr. Williams' services was 81 patients long. We briefly considered another surgeon in Texas, but never had to make that decision. Once Dr. Williams reviewed Tyler's case personally, he decided Tyler should be moved to the top of his wait list.

So, in the blink of an eye, we had moved from S.C. to Atlanta, bought a house that became our home, enrolled three children in new schools, started a new career…and then pushed the pause button. We were in that hospital room the night before surgery with Dr. Williams and a very bleak outlook. We needed a miracle.

It was a long night of stomach aches, tears, and prayers. It was one of those times when you hope and pray for the best but fear the worst. The next morning was difficult, especially when Tyler was rolled away from his hospital room. We composed ourselves and moved to the waiting room where we were astonished to find standing room only—family members, co-workers and friends were there for never-to-be-forgotten support.

We waited and waited and waited. After nine hours, Dr. Williams emerged, shaking his head in disbelief. His words will never be forgotten: "You can learn something every day regardless of how many surgeries you do … your son's heart had the largest hole I have ever seen in a child's heart … " Dr. Williams went on to tell us that the hole was so large that a valve had prolapsed into it, blocking the hole almost entirely and creating the perception on all past image testing that only a tiny hole existed. All of that was wrong. He made a decision during surgery to ease the valve back into its normal position and apply a double patch on the large hole. And he decided against valve replacement. "Let's just let nature take its course from here," he said, "and see what happens."

Well, many grown people cried a lot of tears of relief in that waiting room. Little Tyler was up and walking within 72 hours. The same six-year-old who had not gained a pound in three years added a pound a day for 12 days. And he also found time to encourage a little girl in the hospital room next to him. She needed to walk after her surgery but was too scared even with her parents' encouragement. With Tyler's reassurance, however, the two walked the hall together.

Tyler never needed blood thinners, did not need another surgery, and went on to play baseball, basketball, football, and golf. He repeated an elementary grade after missing school while recovering from the surgery, but he made up that year by getting his college degree in three years. He then earned a law degree, later worked for some of those same guys in his waiting room, and now is married with two beautiful daughters. And a healthy heart.

Dr. Rastegar and Dr. Williams are heroes for sure. But they surely had help from above on this one.

So, do you believe in miracles? We do.

Three Really Bad Words

Trey and I have had quite a few confidential conversations, me the Grandad and him a Grandson. Just the two of us.

A lot of those chats have been at The Cabin, some in a boat, others riding in a vehicle. Of course, what happens at The Cabin stays at The Cabin, and that applies to boats and vehicles as well. But there is a ten-year rule that I forgot to mention to Trey. After ten years, anything goes.

So, Trey is older than 16 now. When he was six—maybe five—we were talking about nothing in particular, when the subject of bad words came up. We were sitting in the den of my Roswell home, and his parents were in another room. Surprisingly, he told me that he knew three bad words. No telling what he had heard at school, on the bus or wherever. I was very curious.

"What are they?" I asked him.

"No way, Grandad," he said. "I can't tell you."

"Why?" I asked.

"My Dad told me to never say those three words," he said. "So, I cannot say them."

My curiosity was getting the best of me. Plus, I was bracing for some pretty rough language.

"Just whisper them to me," I told him.

"No way, Grandad. They are really bad words, and I'm not supposed to say them."

I told him okay and that I was proud of him for not saying bad words and for listening to his parents.

Then Trey had a suggestion. "Maybe if we went in the basement nobody would hear me," he said, adding, "let's go in the basement." Which we did. I suspected Trey didn't mind saying the words in confidence but did not want anybody to know. I braced for some really bad words.

"You're not going to tell anybody, right?" he reaffirmed. I assured him our talk was between the two of us (while not mentioning the ten-year statute of limitations). So, what are the really bad words?

"Well, the first one is stupid. You should never call anybody stupid or even say that someone is stupid," he explained. "Nobody is stupid, Grandad."

I told him he was right and that I totally agree. What about the second bad word?

"Well, the second word is dumb," he said. "Never call anybody dumb or even say somebody is dumb. It's just a bad word."

Okay, now, what about the third bad word?

"It's a really bad word, Grandad. It's loser. Nobody is a loser. Nobody."

Well, besides being very relieved, it occurred to me that my grandson was getting some really good up-bringing at home. I was proud of him but even more proud of his mom and dad.

Before we left the basement, Trey and I agreed to never use the three bad words around others. But we also agreed that it was okay to use them when it was just the two of us. We got a good laugh out of that.

A week later, I picked up Trey for a trip to The Cabin and some fishing. We loaded his gear, strapped him in, and started backing out of his driveway.

"Hey, Grandad," he said. "Don't hit that stupid tree when you are backing out." We both laughed hard.

And just down the street, it was, "I bet that dog is a loser." We laughed even harder.

We enjoyed a lot of really bad words on that trip to The Cabin. Just the two of us.

Three Significant Events

During my newspaper working years in Atlanta, we were required to turn in a monthly report of "Significant Events." Every department, every month.

I often asked myself, just what is considered a truly significant event? Back then, of course, it was all business. Stats, etc. But many of those months I would play a mind game driving home in the traffic and ask myself what has happened … outside of business … that was truly significant.

I recall three such truly significant events. Each involves one of our children, and each continues to be a feel-good memory to this day.

MONICA AND SOCCER

First, a display of determination and grit by our daughter Monica—more than 40 years ago. Youth soccer registration had more than maxed out, and I was asked if I would coach an additional team in the league. I knew zero about soccer—absolutely zero. Didn't even know how many players to put on the field for a game. But the parental hierarchy at Pineview in West Columbia tugged on my conscience about kids who would not get to play, etc. As a bonus, they offered, I would get to have my son AND my daughter on the team.

But wait a minute, wasn't this a soccer league for boys? And Monica had never even played soccer. Well, I read a book about soccer and agreed to coach the team. And Monica agreed to be on the team so we would have enough players, a fact that seemed to rub her the wrong way. So, she listened at practice about fundamentals of the sport and mixed it up with the boys on the field. She was by far the prettiest before practice and the dirtiest after. She was pushed, knocked to the ground, and fouled, but she was feisty and learned the game.

When the day arrived for our first game, the field was muddied by rain and our confidence was not very high. But our team had been taught to play defense. If we couldn't score and the other team didn't score, we'd take them into a shootout in overtime and give ourselves a chance with one-on-one shots against their goalie, a game strategy we emphasized each practice. There was just one problem with that strategy during our first game: Monica was determined to score. And, early in the first half, with several defenders around her—all boys—she slammed a kick into the net for our first goal of the season.

She immediately looked toward the crowd and sideline as if to say, "So there, take that!" The crowd howled with cheers and her proud coach put on his sunglasses on a cloudy day—some dust in his eyes. Monica did not score another goal that season, but she had made her point with her opponents, her teammates, and her coach.

Now, that was a significant event.

'That was for my Mom'

About 30 years ago, our second child and first son was 13 years old and playing youth baseball. He was a very good player, good enough to be selected for the All-Star team for 13-year-olds. However, the coach of the All-Star team for 14-year-old players wanted Dalton to "play up" on his team. When Dalton accepted that invitation, it didn't make any of his friends happy; 14-year-olds didn't think any 13-year-old was good enough, and 13-year-olds were ticked off because he left them.

All of that was bad enough. But adding more stress was the fact that Dalton's Mom (my WW) was to be hospitalized for surgery and would have to miss the All-Star games. It would be the first time she missed any of her children's games in any sport.

Because he was the youngest on the 14-year-old All Star team, Dalton was not a starter. With his team behind by one run with two out in the last inning, Dalton, who had not played in the game, was tapped to pinch hit. His teammates sneered and snickered, and a couple even started to pack their bags. So, with little support from the older players who thought he did not belong on the team, Dalton stepped to the plate and hit the ball out of the park to tie the game. But that was not the significant event.

With his teammates suddenly jubilant and rushing out to greet him at home plate, Dalton calmly circled the bases. When he rounded third base, heading home with the tying run, he stoically barked something to the third-base coach.

After the biggest hit of the tournament and one of the biggest of his life, what on earth could he have said to the third-base coach?

"That was for my Mom," Dalton had said while rounding third base. He wasn't thinking about the game. He wasn't thinking about 14-year-old All Stars or 13-year-old All Stars. He wasn't thinking about being a hero. He was thinking about his mom, who was in the hospital.

Now, that was a significant event.

A Simple Four-Yard Gain

Split end Tyler took a couple of steps up field after the ball was snapped, cut across the middle of the field, put a move on the defender and looked back at the quarterback. The pass was chest high, and he pulled it in for a short gain. No one else in this world remembers that play except Tyler's parents.

Like sister Monica in boys' soccer, Tyler seemed to have a point to prove. He had been told years earlier before heart surgery that he probably would not play contact sports again. Even though his surgery was successful, his parents, somewhat discreetly, had tried to steer him away from playing football. A string bean with no business on a football field, Tyler nonetheless had something to prove — mainly to himself.

When he caught the pass and was tackled for a four-yard gain as a high school freshman in a junior varsity game, Tyler's Mom gasped with a deep sigh of relief. His Dad had to pull his sunglasses down — it was a cloudy day, but something had caused his eyes to water. Yes, a meaningless four-yard gain to everyone else — didn't even result in a first down — but Tyler had made his point. He didn't play football again after that season. He didn't need to.

Now, that was a significant event.

Mocha's Last Ride

When we first saw tiny Mocha, the vet advised us that she was the runt of the litter and therefore might be a little slow in life.

She will be just fine, I assured him, just fine. Besides, we'll just call her Mocha-Mocha in case she doesn't get it the first time.

As things turned out, Mocha was not slow in any way. She even learned to spell much quicker than her peers. When she looked up at you with her wide eyes and barked twice, we knew it spelled "g-o" as in … she wanted to go for a ride. Four distinct barks and there was no doubt she was spelling "w-a-l-k." She was rarely denied, looked forward to her car rides, and wore out a lot of leashes.

Mocha also loved laps and her soft blanket. And small raw carrots and WW's homemade macaroni and cheese … and French fries from McDonald's.

Being the runt of her litter made Mocha feisty. She also was fast, especially when you dropped a tiny morsel of anything edible. You could kiss that morsel goodbye. And if it happened to be a French fry, it never hit the floor.

As chihuahuas go, Mocha was as good as it gets. The only possible comparable was her predecessor, Yoda, who was calm and deliberate and ladylike. Mocha-Mocha would have none of that. More like a tomboy with a devilish gleam when she was up to no good. She knew she shouldn't, but she was going to do it anyway.

Mocha especially enjoyed the long ride to The Cabin — most likely because the ride always meant a stop for McDonald's French fries at Exit 80. No doubt, she could sense when we were nearing that exit. After two fries she would nap in her blanket the rest of the way. She always waited for another fry, but she knew better.

Mocha's 14 years with us followed Yoda's 11. How could we possibly ask for more?

Then the vet told us one Friday to take Mocha home for the weekend in hopes that she would rebound. The look in his eyes said something else: the weekend most likely would be our final couple of days with her. Something had happened, almost suddenly, as she settled down onto her pallet … no more spring in her legs, no gleam in her eyes, only pain. Fourteen years had taken its toll.

So, we took her home for the weekend. Nothing would perk her, not even a dab of WW's macaroni and cheese. She just wanted to rest. So, she slept with us Saturday and Sunday nights although I was awake most of Sunday night, looking at her and asking God to take her gently.

Monday was a sad day. I held a sedated Mocha as the vet gave her the injection. Within seconds she was at peace in my arms and on her way to greet Yoda. Indeed, she was taken gently. The vet suggested cremation, but we already had a site picked for Mocha—she would be buried next to Yoda at The Cabin on the lake.

Mocha's last ride was two hours of sad silence—except at Exit 80 to order French fries. Cuddled in her favorite blanket, she rode in her usual place on the seat next to me. She would be buried in her favorite blanket, snuggled up with her favorite toy, a couple of carrots … and French fries—a double order.

Unlike us, Mocha-Mocha would be just fine.

3. Friends

Friends come from all directions. Some you have known most of your life and others seem to appear unexpectedly. The new ones are treats that come at any age. Old friends seem to stick around to share memories. They are golden — the memories and the friends.

Some friends are couples who renew wedding vows with you after 40 years. Some are former grammar school and high school friends who tap The Cabin as a great reunion venue twice a year. Some are individuals you might have coached nearly 70 years ago. One might have saved your life while becoming a friend. Some are first-time acquaintances on a riverboat cruise who have interesting stories to tell. And some no longer are with us but still a big part of the memories. Maybe all of us should just get busy living and … making more friends.

40-Year Renewal of Vows

Three guys and a plan.

Each of us was near 40 years of marriage. Would there be any possible way we could surprise our wives with a ceremony to renew our wedding vows? It was just a thought at the time back in 2009.

"Well, to begin with, we still have a couple of years to get to 40, and I'm not sure we'll make it," said one of the guys. "She made me pretty mad the other day."

The other's initial reaction: "And, I'm thinking about trading in mine for a newer model. I understand there are some good deals out there."

It should be noted that those remarks were made at a guys-only gathering.

But the seed was planted for a surprise renewal of our vows once all of us passed 40 years of marriage. The seed germinated for a couple years until 2011 when it started to sprout.

Maybe a trip to Hilton Head and somehow surprise them there? The "somehow" was the challenge. I doubt there was any-thing done the past 40 years by any of these guys that was not signed, sealed, and delivered, in advance, by the three wives. So, to surprise all three? We decided to give it a try.

My thoughts kept returning to a beautiful little chapel on the banks of the Red River in Palmetto Bluff, a quaint com-munity in Bluffton, S.C. Palmetto Bluff is a picture-perfect setting not far off Hilton Head Island. The chapel is the site of weddings, receptions, etc. Just across the street is Buffalo's, a restaurant the girls would like. Maybe lunch and then walk over to visit the chapel? The puzzle was starting to take shape, but a big piece was missing. We needed a pastor to administer the vows.

Rev. Martin Lifer was the senior pastor at Providence Pres-byterian in Hilton Head. Even his name had the right ring to it for the occasion. It was an unusual request: three couples, friends since high school, each married 40-plus years, wanting to renew their wedding vows, a surprise service for the wives, probably in the chapel at Palmetto Bluff. After noting the rarity of three couples married for 40 years or more—to the same person no less—Rev. Lifer didn't flinch. Just tell him when and where and it would be his honor.

This plan was coming together, but there was little confi-dence that we could keep the scheme from the girls. October 6,

2011 was set as the date. Rev. Lifer was the minister. The chapel was the place. Two months to go.

The manager at Buffalo's Restaurant—not to be confused with a chicken wings place—thought our idea was awesome. Her only question was one of disbelief, "Forty years … three couples … forty years each?" She would arrange seating for six and be sure one of the guys was facing a window in order to see Rev. Lifer arrive and enter the chapel. That would be the cue.

October 6, 2011, arrived. After getting to Hilton Head the day before, the couples enjoyed a normal coffee-and-breakfast morning at Harbour Town. The plan was in place. Then, a kink. The girls announced they would rather go shopping and save Palmetto Bluff for another day. Blank, panicked stares of fright from the guys. "You can do that if you'd like," I stumbled. "I'll see if we can get reservations at Buffalo's another day." The other two guys swallowed their tongues. Normally, Buffalo's doesn't even take reservations.

The girls decided on their own to stick with the plan to visit Palmetto Bluff as scheduled. They knew only that we had lunch at Buffalo's at 1 p.m. Still knew nothing about a 2 p.m. appointment in the chapel.

The entire Buffalo's staff must have been in on our plan. Never have ordinary customers been treated more royally. "Ladies, we have you seated here, and, gents, you may take your seats," the hostess said, a wink in my direction. The curtain had been positioned so the view of the chapel entrance was clear and direct from my chair. "What a pretty little chapel," said one of the guys, right on script. "Maybe we can check it out after lunch." The girls thought that was a wonderful idea, thank goodness.

Lunch took less than an hour; the staff at Buffalo's saw to that. At 1:45, I noticed Rev. Lifer enter the chapel. We were getting close. The girls powdered their noses after lunch and came outside. They wanted to see the chapel. So, we walked in that direction and up the steps.

Rev. Lifer was waiting inside, down the aisle at the front of the chapel, Bible and notes in hand. "Welcome," he called out, addressing the girls by name. "Come on down. We are here today to celebrate 40 years of marriage—and to renew your vows to each other." Stunned to tears, the girls were caught completely off guard. For the first time in 40 years, all three were speechless. Each couple renewed vows individually and reverently with Rev. Lifer followed by hugs, tears, and cheers (by the guys). The girls were totally surprised, and the guys totally relieved.

So, the good Lord willing, the three couples will hit their magical 50-year anniversaries. Three guys and … another plan?

"I'm not sure we will make it to fifty," said one. "She made me mad the other day."

"I'm thinking about trading mine in for a newer model," said the other.

Well, I know of a pretty chapel on the Red River.

Hero In Houston

Thirteen years ago, my WW (Wonderful Wife) and I were sitting at a table in the dining hall at MD Anderson Cancer

Center in Houston. We were agonizing as we awaited more results of biopsies of a tumor—already diagnosed in Atlanta as malignant—in my neck. We had met Dr. Chris Holsinger a day earlier. I remember wondering if he had started shaving yet.

My WW and I obviously looked distressed as we picked at our salads. Into the dining hall walked a group of doctors including Dr. Holsinger. He caught our worried looks, left his group, and pulled up a chair at our table.

"You look worried," he said. "Let me assure you of something. There is nothing we will encounter that we won't have a plan for. Nothing." He stayed with us for quite a while, encouraging us to eat, but understanding why we couldn't. We learned about his family, and he learned about ours. Then he bopped up and off he went to save lives.

We did not get good news the next day but somehow felt better about facing our challenge with Dr. Holsinger in charge. As we approached surgery, we met several times with him. A couple of things stood out: he was always upbeat, cheerful, and optimistic, and he always had a hug for my WW. Always.

During one of our conversations, I told him I was planning to write a book someday. "If you get me through this tumor thing, you might get a mention in my book," I told him with a smile. He was amused and often asked me in subsequent visits if I had started my book. "Well, I'm still kickin' which means you're still doing a pretty good job … so far. You keep this up and you might move up from a mention to your own sentence, maybe even a paragraph."

I appreciated Dr. Holsinger so much I decided to write a

letter of thanks to him a few months after the surgery. Then I changed my mind and decided to write the letter to his wife. I told her how much my WW and I appreciated her husband, not just his surgical and medical skills but also — mostly — his caring, sincere manner. I told her she was fortunate to have him as a husband. Dr. Holsinger later thanked me for sending the letter and, typically, said he put it on a coffee table in their house in plain view for several days so his wife would not forget the part about how fortunate she is to have him. So it was with this talented but obviously down-to-earth surgeon.

Follow-up visits to Houston became follow-up visits to Palo Alto, California after Dr. Holsinger accepted an offer to become Professor and Chief of Head and Neck Surgery at Stanford University Medical Center. Not surprising at all to us. In not-so-medical terms, he knows his stuff. Our choice was either to stay with M.D. Anderson in Houston or go with Dr. Holsinger to California for on-going scans. Easy decision. After all, he had started shaving by then.

And, after nine years of trips to Houston and three more years to Palo Alto, Dr. Holsinger told us, in so many words, that since I'm still kickin' after 12 years, there's no reason for us to keep meeting like this. We were happy to be released but obviously sad to say farewell. His last act with us was a hug for my WW.

And, that possible mention in my book? Dr. Holsinger had gone from a mention to a sentence to a paragraph to his own chapter. A blog is the least I can do for a hero.

People and Places

Some places are just downright unforgettable. Kinda like some people.

Our Viking riverboat cruise lived up to its billing. We visited The Netherlands, Germany, Austria, and Hungary. Saw castles, cathedrals, and palaces every day. The vineyards outnumbered the glasses of wine we enjoyed, and that's saying a lot.

We visited Amsterdam's Keukenhof Gardens that boasts of six million tulips. I think we saw all of them, but I stopped counting just short of a hundred. Each castle had its own story, each cathedral its own brilliance and each palace its own family history. And I didn't see a single creaky screen door on any of those palaces.

The sites were plentiful and breathtaking. But these trips are as much about the people as the places. Our riverboat, the

Viking Baldur, had rooms to accommodate about 180 of us. Excuse me, staterooms for 180 of us. And, with three unnecessarily lavish meals each day there was plenty of time to eat and meet. Mature adults, i.e., old folks, i.e. us, tend to get clique-ish, especially during a 17-day ride. So, our clique formed quickly with some interesting characters.

Mack, from New Mexico who likes to be called a portion of his last name, is the type guy who could be a friend for life. His real name is Gary and he livens every conversation with a subtle quip that brings belly laughs. A former rugby toughie, he kept studying in life and earned four undergraduate degrees. Sticking a ring on Cathy's finger 25 years ago was his best accomplishment and being part of their 25th anniversary on the riverboat was special. Knew Mack half the cruise before learning he had polio as a child and wore those Forest Gump leg braces. No need to dwell on any of that. "Always better to look forward than backward," he says. Quality guy; quality wife.

James and Lynn have been married twice as long as Mack and Cathy. From Arkansas, this couple is celebrating 50 years of marriage by tripping to several places around the world. Either could have stepped off the pages of a fashion magazine, but Lynn was not shy about wearing the anniversary gift from new riverboat friends — plastic, gaudy, pierced diamond earrings. We worried her ear lobes might turn green after the third day. This couple fit right in.

John and Marcia, from California, found a place at our table most meals, too. I had to prod John to remove his blue LA

Dodgers hat a couple of times. His response: "Do you guys play major league baseball in Atlanta?" They fit right in, too.

Leaders of the pack were the Brewers, our traveling partners and S.C. friends forever. Buddy, who uses "awesome" to describe everything, probably met 179 of the 180 passengers. Wife Lynn could teach the Viking cruise managers and tour guides a thing or two. As a couple, the Brewers are … well, awesome.

Outside our clique were other interesting people. There was the gregarious businesswoman executive from Pennsylvania who previously had been a nun for 25 years. And the beef and hay manufacturer from Utah. And the nice couple who recently had moved from Hawaii to Georgia and now live in Marietta—just a short distance from our home in Woodstock. We went halfway around the world to meet these neighbors.

There were others, too, but by far the most interesting couple we met on board was Leonard and Mary Ann, from Oregon. Leonard, a lawyer, has authored 30-plus books and is busy on nine revisions. Supreme Court Justice Ruth Bader Ginsburg penned a forward for one of his books, as did several other notables. Leonard and Mary Ann have been on 32 cruises since 2002, and they schedule two every year despite working full-time. They met in 1964 and have been married 52 years. But they do not talk about 1964. Leonard is blind, and 1964 is when he lost part of his left arm, fingers on his right hand and his eyesight. When he was brought to the hospital, Mary Ann was his nurse who promised to stay by his side during his recovery. She has been his eyes ever since. He has never seen her. And that's all they have to say about that.

Kinda like Mack said, always better to look forward than backward. Even if you cannot see.

For 17 days, Leonard and Mary Ann trudged through castles, gazed at sky-high cathedrals, and visited ornate mansions with gold walls and meticulously detailed ceilings and artwork. And he is blind. With his right hand seemingly attached to her shoulder, she continuously and quietly described details for him to envision. Whether through windows on a bus ride or from the top deck of the Baldur, Mary Ann was Leonard's eyes with a patient description for everything. How amazing.

At breakfast one morning, Leonard talked about the cabin they own on a river in Oregon. He described details of each room, confirmed by Mary Ann's photos, even though he has never seen the cabin. We swapped cabin stories and agreed that we should plan trips to visit each other—at our cabins. Such a special, inspiring couple.

The Viking cruise concluded in Budapest, one of the world's most photographed cities. A night cruise along the Danube produced spectacular views of the city, sites that are downright unforgettable.

Kinda like the people.

DMC: Six-Day Weekend

The three-day weekend became a six-day weekend.

It started as a Friday-to-Sunday fishing event, but the first guys will arrive this year on Tuesday and farewells will be Sunday. A semblance of golf will be played Wednesday, Thursday, and Friday—if the bodies hold up. Saturday will be a day to rejuvenate muscles, watch college football, and plop several racks of ribs on the fire pit.

Every evening the ritual is the same: sit around the fire ring outside and embellish the same stories that have been repeated year after year.

Stories like the year we had fishing competition only to discover one guy was considering buying frozen fish from the local grocery and entering them. Some stories are sort of true, some half true. Never heard one that is truly true. But everybody hurts every year from laughing. That's the truth.

The tie that binds this group is Eau Claire High School in Columbia, S.C. All guys are 1965 high school grads—five from EC and one a stray from Dentsville HS who qualified for admission by marrying an EC girl. That stray is Smit. The others in the group are aptly called Redman, Bud Lite, Weeble, Crampey and yours truly Little Richard. The names kinda indicate the fun we've been having the past 20 years at The Cabin. Once a year, first week in November, be there.

The origin of our get-together reaches back to the late 1990's. Another high school classmate, Danny Mann, would meet me at The Cabin for some fishing back then. Bud Lite and Redman joined us about a year later as the group began to grow. Then Danny died suddenly in 2004. From that year forward, we called our annual gathering the Danny Mann Classic (DMC). Each year, the extra-long weekend concludes Sunday morning on the waterfront as everybody hits a golf ball into the lake in memory of our good friend Danny.

Arrival at a DMC is like kids on Christmas morning. Everybody brings something for everybody else—monogrammed DMC hats, shirts, golf towels, golf balls. And snacks, goodness, enough snacks to stock a Kroger—even though everybody is well aware of the annual menu lineup.

Wednesday dinner is a low country boil—shrimp, sausage, corn on the cob, red potatoes all in a big pot; Thursday, smoked beer-butt chicken, and sausage; Friday, thick steaks on the fire pit; and Saturday, fire pit ribs compliments of Redman, our master chef. One guy suggested quiche, but he hasn't been seen since. Breakfasts are obscenely large, and evening desserts are aplenty, highlighted by Smit's personal, popular concoction: Krispy Kreme doughnuts topped with Neapolitan ice cream, M&M's, marshmallows, syrupy walnuts, chocolate syrup, a red cherry, whipped cream and finished off with colorful sprinkles. True.

Despite all this healthy eating, each of us made it to our seventies. Amazing, but most of us have been friends for more than 60 of those years, stretching back to elementary school. The bonds have been strengthened by significant events such as life-threatening cancer battles, major heart surgery, the loss of parents, the birth of children, and the birth of grandchildren—not to mention multiple replacements of hips, shoulders, and knees. Orthopedic surgeons appreciate this group.

Highlights of these DMC gatherings are many, but a couple are noteworthy. Danny Mann's 84-year-old dad joined us in 2006. Said he wanted to see first-hand why Danny enjoyed the gathering so much. He shared several stories, which made him a natural for the group. He once built a gyrocopter by hand, crashed it on its maiden flight, but survived to tell about it. We always called him Gyro after that, and we all attended Gyro's funeral a couple years after he attended his first DMC.

There's also the continuing saga about The Four Lasses, a singing group in our high school senior class. Every time we tried to remember the names of the Four Lasses; we came up with five names. The closest we can come to a resolution is that there must have been five Four Lasses. Anyway, we always agree to think about it for another year. We'll figure it out.

And there's the case of the disappearing new pontoon. It was safely tied up in its boathouse slip all day but then it was gone early that evening. Just gone. Vanished. Just before calling law enforcement, one of the guys spotted it with binoculars in the corner of a nearby cove. An attempted theft or a prank? Little doubt in my mind that a couple of the guys conspired with a neighbor named Bill. But, years later nobody is near a confession, and everybody is a laughing suspect.

As our age continues to progress (i.e., we're getting old), we seem to appreciate these outings—and each other—even more. Not coincidentally, one of the guys suggested last year that perhaps it would be wise to start meeting twice a year. So, the Mini DMC was born.

It will start as a three-day weekend.

Paul and Pope Davis

I always knew Paul would do well.

My first team as a youth baseball coach was Pope Davis, named after a tire company in West Columbia, S.C. The team had a reputation for not winning. As I recall, rules in the Pineview league required players to stay on the same team each year until their age prompted a move up to the next league. Well, Pope Davis had not won a game in two years, maybe three. Opposing teams liked to play the Pope Davis team I inherited.

Odd, but I can recall names of the five- and six-year-olds on that first team. Brian at first, Kevin at second, Dalton at shortstop, Phillip at third, John in left field, Torrey in center, Michael in right, Scott behind home plate and Samantha on the mound. But where was Paul? The lineup of nine left no position for Paul at the start of the season. He was our first sub. A sub with a smile.

We emphasized fundamentals the first year. My theory has always been that no kid ever allows a grounder to go through his legs intentionally, so there's never a reason to yell after an error. The kid already feels bad enough; just teach him fundamentals so it might not happen the next time. On the other hand, nothing is wrong with a polite holler to Torrey in centerfield, who is trying to catch a grasshopper, or to John in left field, who is mesmerized by a plane in the sky. Both true memories.

So, fundamentals helped Pope Davis win a game the first season, several the second season and — get this — go 16-0 the third season. That's the year nobody wanted to play Pope Davis. But, what about Paul?

While Paul was not a starter in his first game for Pope Davis, it was obvious that he was a smart kid—very smart—who always had an enthusiastic attitude, a zest for the game, and a smile. He could not run very fast, probably the slowest on the team, but nobody out-hustled him and nobody improved faster. And he learned to hit the cover off the ball.

Paul became a starter after just a couple of games. He first mastered the outfield, then third and second base and then shortstop. Before the first season ended, he could play any position. Coaches did the pitching, or he probably could have done that as well. More on that later. He was picked as an All-Star at the end of the second and third seasons.

The Pope Davis experience was one of those worst-to-first tales. That's probably why the names and memories are still fresh after 37 years. Pretty sure Samantha was the first girl to play in the league; Torrey was probably the first black player, and his brother Kelsey joined us the second year; Scott walked into a swinging bat at practice, lost his front teeth and spent the evening at the emergency room. My most vivid memory: an outfielder at practice would not come off the field so I went out to get him only to hear "Coach, I pooped in my pants." I have never summoned a mother to the field so fast.

Shortly after the Pope Davis days, we moved to the Atlanta area and lost touch with most of our West Columbia area players and their parents. But the memories of that first team still ring clear. And, what about Paul?

Paul went on to be an outstanding player at Lexington High School before playing one year at Clemson University as a pitcher (1.50 earned run average) and then three seasons at Vanderbilt University where he won 14 games as a starting pitcher. It did not end there. He was a pitcher in the Boston Red Sox organization where he played for the Gulf Coast Red Sox team as a relief pitcher in 130 games. He recorded 196 strikeouts in 220 innings pitched. Not bad for a slow-footed kid who did not start for a winless Pope Davis team as a six-year-old.

But it doesn't end there for Paul either. If you Google the name Paul Seybt, you will find M.D. after his name. He's with a group of doctors who provide pathology services at Lexington Medical Center. Dr. Paul Seybt is the one with the smile.

I always knew Paul would do well.

That Quirky Phone Call

Woodstock was defined by a railroad track, a pharmacy, and an antique shop back in 1987 when we first moved to Georgia. Today, Chamber of Commerce marketeers use "vibrant" and "booming" to describe it.

We settled in Roswell back in '87 and were about five miles from Woodstock. That's when the road connecting the two towns was a very narrow two lanes. We loved our Roswell home, reared our three children there, and established forever memories. Didn't think we would ever consider moving, but 26 years later we did. Our younger son bought the house, changed his name etched on the tree house to the name of his first daughter, and we were all happy the homestead stayed in the family.

All of that left us somewhat anxious about a move to Woodstock or anywhere else eight years ago. But my WW had kept her eye on a small, picturesque neighborhood tucked away in downtown Woodstock. The quaint neighborhood was somewhat hidden behind an old-fashioned Ace Hardware. We picked out a couple of lots overlooking a big park and were ready to draw plans for a down-sized home and yard. Those plans did not materialize, but that futile exercise only energized our interest in the neighborhood—called Hedgewood years ago and Woodstock Downtown today.

A quirky phone call actually led us to our Woodstock home.

We were on a Sunday-afternoon ride that took us to Woodstock and the twisting streets behind the Ace. That's when we saw a For Sale sign on a house on Hubbard Road. We pulled into a parking space directly in front of the house. "Let's call and ask about it," my WW said, pointing to the cell number on the For Sale sign. "The salesperson's name is Carol." Homes were difficult to get in this particular area of Woodstock, so we knew we should act quickly.

Carol immediately answered her phone. After getting a few

details, I asked if we could possibly see the inside of the house and, if so, when. "How about right now," Carol said, the perfect answer. As it turned out, Carol was the next door neighbor to this same house. She was sitting on her porch and talking on her cell phone—to us. We waved to her, ended our call, and met on the sidewalk.

And that's how we found our Woodstock home.

Carol had lots of good advice for us, moreso as a neighbor than our real estate agent. She told us that front porches are important in the neighborhood so be sure to make ours attractive because many neighbors would pass by daily while taking their walks. And, one other thing.

"It's not as important to remember your neighbors' names as it is to remember the names of their dogs," she advised. So, over time, we have gotten to know neighbors Chelsea, Louie, Stella, Sophie, Chloe, Mugs and Ransom—the canines. Their owners are pretty interesting neighbors, too, and we met a lot of them while sitting on our front porch.

Chelsea's parents, Brian and Sylvia, bought Carol's house—real estate people do a lot of that. Brian might as well be on our payroll. He retrieves our mail, trash receptacles and packages when we're at The Cabin or elsewhere, which is often. He also witnessed a miracle one day: a FedEx truck passed by without stopping to deliver a package for my WW.

Louie and Stella take Tim for walks at least twice a day. Tim has orange blood, a member of the 1981 Clemson national championship football team. His wife Julia is a jewel, does my WW's hair, and I have told her many times that she can do better than Tim. But they are bound for life; she bleeds orange, too.

Also on Hubbard Road are Mugs, a schnauzer who belongs to Sheb and Cynthia, and Taylor's "Little Man" Ransom, a tea cup chihuahua. Mugs has one of the prettiest yards in which to roam and do other things. Ransom has Taylor wrapped around his paw and a huge courtyard in which to sniff. You can be sure that whatever Ransom wants, Ransom gets. Taylor, a retired Delta flight attendant after 50 years, brings a sercie for my WW every time she visits. I reciprocate with smoked ribs from The Cabin or a bag of fresh boiled peanuts. Good chance the sercies will continue as long as the ribs do.

The mail truck stops every day for chihuahuas Sophie and Chloe two houses down from us where Michael and Pam live. The mailman stops so Sophie can jump in and get her daily tour of the mail truck. Michael's middle names are golf and Coke. He asked me to join his golf foursome soon after we moved in, and the camaraderie is always better than the golf. A Coca Cola retiree, Michael would prefer warm water rather than Pepsi.

The front side of our house allowed us to meet Hubbard Road neighbors as we often sat on our porch in the afternoons with our iced tea (also called Riesling). Our decks off the back of the house are ideal for morning coffee and watching non-retirees pull out of their garages on their way to work. We smile; they frown. Alley life is fun and the alley introduced us to yet another round of neighbors.

Curt and his wife Patt previously owned our house. They

liked the neighborhood so much, they stayed. Their home is only half a block away, just down the alley in the back. Curt became a best buddy even though he often bemoans the deal we struck when signing closing papers for the house. It's the same conversation every time after I remind him that we paid him his full asking price.

"You got a deal," he'd say. "And it was move-in ready, but you changed everything in the house. Every inch." Then I would remind him that I had not touched the mailbox. Yet. Curt's familiar laugh always followed.

Curt and I covered a lot of ground on our exercise jaunts through Woodstock and while playing golf. And it wasn't just the geography we covered. If the world would just listen, chances are good Curt and I could solve a lot of today's problems.

Other friends on the alley include Jeff and Margaret, David and Melissa and Danny and Janie. Jeff and I have remained friends even after I backed into his Kia and created a chain reaction of repair headaches for him. David and Melissa are our alarm clocks, or at least their sports cars are when they crank and pull out each morning. But David is a town councilman so nobody complains.

Danny and Janie live next to Curt and Patt. Janie is a hoot, a really good hoot who loves cats, especially Boots the feline orphan who's no longer an orphan thanks to you know who. Janie nearly scared the wits out of all the neighborhood the year she dressed up like a witch on Halloween.

Danny, Patt's brother and the purest golfer in our foursome, grew up in the same neighborhood as Elvis. Yes, that's Elvis Pressley. Retired airline pilots and brothers-in-law, Danny and Curt could write a book about their experiences. And Taylor, the retired flight attendant, could pen a chapter or two of her own. She's babysat Art Linkletter, Lucille Ball, Farrah Fawcett, Muhammad Ali, Wilt Chamberlain, Angelina Jolie, Jerry Lewis, Barbara Mandrell and the AC/DC rock band on various flights.

Yes, interesting neighbors in a desirable area that circles a big park. But it's still mostly hidden with courtyards and buckling sidewalks while the town grows around it.

That road connecting Woodstock to Roswell has grown to six lanes and is packed daily. The Hot Dog Heaven joint might be gone, but Woodstock Downtown now has at least 15 eating establishments within walking distance of our home. Miles and miles of elaborate walking trails have been cleared and paved for the public—and for dogs. Entertainment spots and sports bars have sprung up. At last count, five ice cream shops have opened. And now, of all things, even the old-fashioned Ace Hardware will be moving. Rumor has it that the downtown area needs a boutique hotel, and Ace's corner is the desired location.

Woodstock is an old town continuing to become new, but nobody in our quaint neighborhood is complaining. Interesting neighbors, good friends, good dogs. Lots of pooper scoopers.

That quirky phone call ... a good move.

Golf Curse in Disguise

The weather forecast called for back-to-back days with high temperatures of 99. That meant a heat index of nearly 106 degrees.

And we wanted to play golf.

More specifically, it was Member-Guest Tournament time at Columbia Country Club. Long-time friend Charles had asked me to be his guest. Charles obviously was a glutton for punishment in a couple of ways—the heat would be a matter of survival, and I'm not a very good golfer.

But we decided to do it. Just like the previous year when we did not learn our lesson. At least Charles lived within a reasonable distance of the CCC course; I had to travel 248 miles from Woodstock, Georgia to get there. A true glutton for punishment. When will we learn our lesson?

The format for the tournament was fairly simple. Each team would play five nine-hole matches with 20 points at stake in each match. The top teams in each flight (10 flights) would advance to a playoff for the championship. Flights were based on ability—in our case, inability; we were in flight 10. But we were not at all deterred by our low ranking. We had played a respectable practice round the day before; more than that, we were eternal optimists.

Our first match was against a big-bellied guy whose partner was a string bean with power. We held our own and tied these guys 10-10. They eventually would advance to the championship round. We eventually would not.

Our second match was at 12:30. Had that been 12:30 just after midnight, we might have done better. But it was just after noon when the temperature had risen, and our energy had fallen. We knew we were in trouble when these two flat-bellied youngsters addressed us as "sir." The match wasn't close. I conveniently forget the score. But we had three matches remaining the next day: 9:30, 12:30 and hot-as-hades 2:30. For some totally unknown reason, we continued to be optimistic. Maybe the gallons of Gatorade had impaired our thinking.

The next morning, there we were, waiting to meet our next opponents. Charles and I had wondered if the heat could be a danger for us—two 70-plus-year-olds. Then we met our opponents. One of these guys was so tall I didn't think he would ever stop getting out of his cart. "Good morning, sir," he said. It was the "sir" thing again, but we quickly moved past that when we learned his profession. He was a stent salesman. As in heart stents.

But that wasn't all. Tall Man's partner was a former Irmo High School jock who played football at the University of South Carolina. His profession? He was a pacemaker salesman. "You wouldn't happen to have a couple of those with you, would you?" I asked. He laughed, but we didn't. Charles and I wondered if the country club pro had a medical reason for pairing us with them.

Anyway, Tall and Taller could hit the ball really far but not very straight, and we actually beat them. And, ahem, the score was 14-6 as old age prevailed. Forget the points system. That made us a very respectable 1-1-1 for the tournament. But not for long.

The 12:30 pairing had us against Brooks Koepka and his iron-bellied partner. Brooks, by the way, is a pro golfer who has won the U.S. Open, the PGA Championship, and several other professional tournaments. Our opponent's real name was John, but he was a Brooks lookalike, and, unfortunately for us, he hit the ball much like Brooks. We should have known; these two youngsters were perfectly polite to their elders and also called us "sir" the entire time. As in, "nice shot, sir," which always was a lie. They beat us like a drum. Again, I conveniently forget the score, but Brooks Koepka and his partner advanced to the playoffs.

Well, we knew we had pretty much blown our slim chances to win it all, but we still had one match to go. "We play Jay in our 2:30 match," Charles said optimistically. "We could breeze by these guys." Jay unfortunately had a heart attack a couple weeks earlier, had a stent put in, and was scheduled for heart surgery in a couple of weeks. I was somewhat conflicted about trying to beat a recent heart patient who is also a future heart patient, but we should not have let any of that influence us. They were only nine years younger and did not refer to us as "sir".

The 2:30 heat didn't get us, but Jay, the heart patient, did. He put on one of the best performances of the tournament for the first five holes—par, birdie, par, birdie, par. Our boat had sunk. "Mathematically, we've already lost this match," I told Charles with four holes remaining. "But we should not give up. Let's drink another couple bottles of Gatorade and give it our best." Incredibly, we won the last four holes. Which, no doubt, was a curse in disguise.

After the impressive but futile comeback, Charles surmised, "You know, we could have been in the playoff and won this whole thing; maybe next year." Goodness knows, I think he was serious.

A couple of gluttons for punishment. Yes sir, sir.

Get Busy Living Or

"Get busy living or get busy dying," Andy told Red before escaping prison and a life sentence in the movie The Shawshank Redemption.

We were approaching the 50th anniversary of our high school graduation, and I volunteered to help in any way. The "in any way" is what got me in trouble.

The reunion committee for the Eau Claire High School class of 1965 already was in place and making preparations. Things were coming together nicely, but there was one area that needed some help. The phone call came from a committee member: "We've decided you would be perfect for necrology; you know, with your newspaper background and all."

Necrology. I Googled it to be sure. I was right. I never should have gone into the newspaper business. And I should never blindly volunteer. My reunion job was to come up with a list of classmates who no longer were with us. How depressing. Surely the job nobody wanted.

Our graduating class included 276 graduates if I remember correctly. Previous reunions had produced a list of those who had died since we all tossed our caps in the air at Township Auditorium on Taylor Street. From the information already available, 41 classmates had died prior to our 45th reunion. My job was to update the list the five years since then.

Compiling the list of names was not easy. Word of mouth from classmates was the best source. And comparing notes with Christina Stevens Kirby of the class of 1964 was another valuable source. But after hearing about various discrepancies and uncertainties, I decided it would be best to include those former classmates for whom I could find a published obituary. And some interesting developments occurred along the way. For example, one classmate who was deceased at the 45th reunion was alive and kicking for the 50th reunion. And a couple of others had not been kicking at all for several years, so they were added to the dreaded list.

As the 50th reunion approached, the necrology list had grown to 50 with the verification of death of each, even though a few never had obituaries published. So, our class was averaging exactly one death per year since our graduation in 1965. Then a member of the reunion planning committee died unexpectedly one week before the reunion. So, after 50 years, we had logged 51 deaths.

As our class looks toward our 57th reunion in 2022, the loss rate for our class has increased dramatically with 26 additional deaths so far during the seven years since the 50th reunion. The increase is natural as we age, but losing a classmate always is difficult under any circumstances.

When putting together a 50th reunion booklet with a page for each deceased classmate, I often paused to recall memories related to those no longer with us. I told everybody attending the reunion that they did not want a page in my book and to take care until the next reunion. But I'll reluctantly add 26 pages before we gather again … and hopefully no more than that.

If there's a message in all of this, it's simply about our time on earth. And maybe Andy had it right in The Shawshank Redemption.

Get busy living or …

4. Youth

The innocence of youth might best be captured in written memories. Did it really matter how many games were won by Ridgewood Oil Co. sixty-five years ago? It was the fun that mattered then and maybe not realized until now. How long does it take to realize that a strict high school principal really was your best friend? How did the thrills of yesteryear become dangers of today? What does it mean to sing along with music from sixty-five years ago but have no recollection of last year's top songs? A four-line poem is much different from the dialect version of a 32-liner, but both can tote lifetime insights. Read on ...

A Ton of Fun

We weren't very good. But we had a ton of fun. It didn't take much to figure that out.

Ridgewood Oil Co. was my first baseball team. At least, it was the first team that was truly organized with uniforms and in a league. I often tried to put together a sandlot game with neighborhood friends, but we could not always find a bat or ball or yard big enough to mark off the bases. And, finding the bases themselves could be a challenge—we'd use a rock or hat, or somebody would volunteer their shoes and play barefooted.

But we didn't have to worry about any of that when we

played for Ridgewood Oil. The field was just off Westwood Drive on the grounds of Heyward Gibbes School. The bases were real. Home plate was real. Real umpires. The base paths were straight and marked neatly with white chalk. On game day, we had died and gone to baseball heaven. Didn't matter that most likely we would lose to another team in our league.

Our uniforms were treasures. Some guys might have had to borrow a teammate's hat or glove on game day, but nobody ever misplaced their Ridgewood Oil Co. shirt—unless at the end of the season when all equipment and uniforms had to be turned in. Guys thought it was a badge of honor to be caught wearing a team shirt at school weeks after the season.

The land behind our ball field eventually became a street with several new homes. A friend for many years, Fred Best, and his parents and two older sisters moved into one of those new homes and was the envy of many of us. Fred had a pretty house, pretty yard and … pretty sisters. The field we played on did not have an outfield fence. That meant you could run forever if you could hit the ball between the outfielders and toward Fred's house.

While a lot of those days and facts in the 1950's with Ridgewood Oil are a blur, lots of memories are distinct. Especially memories of teammates. While I could use some help remembering all players on Ridgewood Oil, I do remember most of the guys.

Skip Clark was probably the best player on the team. Good glove, good arm, good hit, as coaches would say. Skip did not win a lot of games for us but only because Ridgewood Oil did not win a lot of games. Heyward Sutherland was our best pitcher and his dad just might have owned Ridgewood Oil—that's one of those blurs. Then there is Jerry Cannon, the smallest player on the team who lived just up our street on Margrave for a while. I remember Jerry's glove being his best asset. Donnie Jeffcoat, one of the best catchers ever in youth ball and beyond in the Eau Claire area. Mostly because of the position he played, Donnie stayed dirty a lot. Donnie's brother Jerry was on the team, too, an outfielder as I recall and the fastest runner on the team no doubt. Kerry Brown, a couple years younger than me, also played as an outfielder. Alvin Loupe was slightly taller than our bat boy, quick and always had tons of energy. Seems like his mouth ran a lot, too.

Larry Dodd and Skip were our best players, and I recall that Larry could knock the ball all the way to Fred's house. Often, he would keep running after hitting it toward Fred's yard even though our base running coaches would holler for him to stop. The bat boy for the team was my brother Harry, and the coach was my dad. Harry didn't really have much to do. He was along mostly for the ice cream cone after the games. Me? Good glove, fair arm, no hit, as the coaches would say.

While I cannot recall names of the other teammates, I do remember that a couple of them were real rascals who would just as soon be elsewhere on game day. Probably lawyers or politicians or incarcerated today.

Game day for Ridgewood Oil Co. was always special. No worries about homework or chores—things required of kids back then. And, despite only one car per family in most cases, players generally were at the field on time. A lot of them, like me, walked a mile or two to the field and arrived in plenty of time.

My dad usually came straight from work to the field with the equipment bag in his trunk. The big stress came if the equipment bag was late; everybody used one of only two or three bats in the bag. Nobody toted their own personal bags with personal helmet, personal batting gloves, personal water bottle and a couple of personal bats. Are you kidding? We never knew what we didn't have.

But if you were on the Ridgewood Oil Co. team, you had a ton of fun.

Margrave and Thrill Hill

It was Highlawn Avenue before it was Margrave Road, but it was best known as Thrill Hill.

Our house number was 4018 and it's the boyhood home I remember most. We moved in back in the fifties when the street name was Highlawn. For some reason the city decided to change the name to Margrave. I do not remember when or why that decision was made, but what difference did it make? The street would forever be known as Thrill Hill anyway.

Thrill Hill attracted hot-rodders nearly every evening. Our house was located at the end of Margrave where the pavement ended and a steep dirt-road drop-off began. Cars, usually with souped-up engines or maybe just souped-up mufflers, would get a half-block running start, fly off the end of the pavement and slam down after being airborne a couple of seconds. Then they would struggle to make it up to Duke Avenue before police could arrive. I guess there wasn't much to do back then in the evenings.

Many times, friends of mine would confess in a whisper the next day at school, "Hey, did you hear me last night?" Never told my parents any names.

Thrill Hill isn't my only memory of Margrave.

Next door for several years was a character named Bill Carroll. A nice neighbor and dad of three who thought he could sing. Sometimes he would practice on his front porch. He could not sing. I get this off my chest now because I'm pretty sure Bill has departed earth by now and cannot be offended. I love my boyhood church, Ridgecrest Baptist, but I will never forgive it for allowing Bill Carroll to sing solos. I think that's why my dad quit going to church. Apologies to any of Bill's surviving children.

Next to the Carrolls was a house we called The Alamo. The Brooks family lived in that fortress-looking place—white stucco walls with a flat roof. Very odd for our day. Expected to see Davy Crockett firing his musket from that rooftop any day. Carol Brooks was the oldest kid living in The Alamo, and he was the meanest kid on Margrave, maybe in all of Eau Claire. He once bloodied my nose for no reason; when my older brother confronted him, Carol bloodied his nose, too. After that, my brother and I would always walk across the street to avoid passing directly in front of The Alamo. My guess is Carol and his younger brother, just as mean, grew up to be professional boxers.

Not everybody on Highlawn left bruising memories. The Davis family was across from The Alamo. Bob was the dad in the family. He worked in produce, spent a lot of time at the Farmers Market, and kept us supplied with bushel baskets of butter beans and crowder peas. My siblings and I didn't like seeing those bushel baskets arrive. No playing until every bean was shelled. But we did enjoy eating those fresh beans and peas.

You did not have to wander far off Margrave to find friends. At the corner of Abingdon and Jackson was a house full of Manleys. Deborah and Susan spent a lot of their time on softball fields, I recall, as All-Stars. Classmate Joanna Wiles was just up Abingdon and not far from the Hemming clan (whatever happened to Linda Hemming?). A house full of Garris boys was on the same side of Abingdon, including Julius, Johnny, and others. Julius and I were pals.

Jay Barry was near the bottom of Myles Avenue not far from Heyward Gibbes School. Jay achieved his childhood goal in life of becoming a fireman only to die while bravely fighting a fire in Eau Claire. Another classmate in Heaven, Doris Murray, also lived on Abingdon. The world lost one of the best when Doris died.

On the other side of Margrave, I could go see Mike Whatley on the corner of Jackson and Ridgewood Avenue. Mike and I were buddies for a long time. Catty-corner from Mike was Phil Forrester's house, and catty-corner from Phil was a house full of Belfords on Johnson Avenue—Eddie, Richie, Linda, Johnnie, Bitsie. Linda and I graduated together in 1965 from Eau Claire

High School. Her family would take up nearly a full pew every Sunday at Ridgecrest where Phil's dad was the preacher.

Diane Kyzer also lived on Margrave in a house and yard as prim and proper as Diane herself. Farther down was Trudie Harris, the Moore girls (Patsy and Judy), and brother Freddie, a house full of Barbees (Betty, Bobby, Billy, and Helen), and the Crout boys (Marvin and Ricky).

I know neighborhoods still exist today with neighborhood friends, but I cannot imagine those having as much fun now with the popularity of iPads, iPhones, and computers. So much time is taken away from the outdoors. Then again, this blog is fueled by my iPad, iPhone, and computer, and such technology has led to many re-connections with old friends (let's make that former friends). I might never had known that Mike Whatley is CEO of a high-end equestrian clothing store not far from me today, Trudie Harris is still singing and dancing, the Barbees are still a close-knit family now populated with grandkids, Marvin Crout and his wife live near the S.C. coast also with grandkids, and Marvin's brother Rick has been hanging around Florida when not piloting airplanes. Heck, Google Earth can even show that Thrill Hill has been paved.

And I don't need technology to tell me that, bless his soul, Bill Carroll is probably singing off key in Heaven where the Good Lord might be considering a transfer for him. I'm not sure I want to hear from the boxing Brooks brothers; they could be a long, long way from Heaven or still on Highlawn Avenue.

Make that Margrave Road. Better still, Thrill Hill.

Art Baker One-On-One

The world needs more Art Bakers. And maybe a Paul Stephens.

We had big issues and worries like the Vietnam War and integration back in the sixties. And, we had challenges with really bad habits like smoking cigarettes and sneaking a beer or, for the really bad teens, taking a swig of liquor. Drugs? You do mean Goody's headache powders, right?

Our everyday struggles and challenges for the most part were not serious because they were not allowed to be. That's because we had parents who whipped our rear-ends when they needed to be whipped and disciplined us when we needed to be disciplined.

And, we had our role models although we might not have known it at the time.

Eau Claire High School was stocked with teachers, coaches, and principals who kept us on the straight and narrow in the sixties. Mr. Hafner and successor Paul Stephens automatically had our respect because they were principals. Note the "Mr." in front of Hafner but the "Paul" in front of Stephens. Maybe a transition of respect was starting during that time, and we didn't even know it. Regardless, both had the respect—and fear—of every student, especially those called to "the office."

A teacher once sent me to "the office" to fetch something. Paul Stephens saw me walk in and, in his booming voice, hollered, "Huguley, what in the world are you doing here?" I had hoped that was the end of attention directed at me, but it wasn't. Then, the never to be forgotten words: "Huguley, tell me, do you have to squat to tee-tee?" It was one of his favorite sayings and most people had heard it before. I couldn't help but laugh, like others in the office, before darting out the door as quickly as possible. That was Paul Stephens—undoubtedly a respected principal and, in his own way, a respected role model.

The best role model at Eau Claire, however, was Coach Art Baker. Few today could argue that Baker has impacted more lives in a positive way than anyone else at Eau Claire High School (and many other places, too).

Baker was the head football coach. He assembled a staff of assistants who were not just top-notch football coaches but also examples of the way life should be lived: Steve Robertson, Jimmy Satterfield, Dick Sheridan, Frank Singleton, Les Evans, Leonard Shealy. Bobby Johnson and others came later. There's no telling how many lives of youngsters were positively changed because of these coaches, all influenced in a big way by Baker.

Baker was not just a coach, although he was highly skilled enough to be head football coach at Furman University, The Citadel, and East Carolina. He also served in assistant roles at Clemson, Texas Tech, and Florida State before retiring after being Associate Athletic Director at the University of South Carolina for nearly seven years. Baker resides in Sumter with his wife Edie, and while his athletics trail ended at USC, the shadow of his excellence as a role model will forever be long.

"When the going gets tough, the tough get going," he would often say before football practices and games at Eau Claire. Every Shamrock player would take on a tractor trailer for their coach. He would never sugarcoat it; football was tough, and life was going to be tough. You just had to be tougher. But always by the rules and always with good sportsmanship. And that's how his teams played.

Baker helped shape lives with regular doses of honesty and integrity, but he was fierce as a competitor. Very fierce. He and his assistant coaches often would meet in the Eau Claire gym after school for a "friendly" basketball scrimmage. That's when the EC gym still had half-moon backboards. Occasionally, these coaches would tap a student to fill in so the teams would be equal in number. One day I was tapped, and the experience still rings clear. It was a one-on-one encounter that would hurt that day but help in another one-on-one another day.

Taking on Coach Baker on the basketball court was a bruising physical experience. I got the best of him a few times that day with the help of slaps on his arms and wrists, and he was good at reciprocating. There were no referees and neither of us was apt to call fouls on ourselves. Finally, his frustration level exceeded mine and emotions boiled over. We shook hands afterwards, but our skirmish was witnessed by many coaches and students. And word of it spread.

Later in the school year, after asking a teacher to please repeat a question in class, the teacher asked if I had washed my ears out that morning. This teacher had a reputation for being rude to students and seemed to enjoy embarrassing them. When I responded, simply and politely, that yes indeed I had washed out my ears, the reply or my tone was not what she wanted to hear. So, she challenged if I would like to go to "the office" and discuss this matter with the principal, Mr. Stephens.

Imagine her shock when I stood up and said, "Sure, let's go" as I headed toward the door.

The conversation with principal Stephens was decidedly one-sided as the teacher presented her version of the incident. Students rarely won such one-on-ones with teachers back in the sixties. She finished by reminding Stephens that this was the same student who also had a run-in with Coach Baker in the gym. Stephens later talked to Baker about the basketball incident and was told the only person out of line that day weeks ago in the gym was a coach who let his emotions get the best of him because, "I was getting my tail whipped." (Coach Baker always used "tail" instead of other more impolite words to describe someone's rear-end. I think his favorite bad word was dadgummit.)

Well, all ended well except for the teacher after the ear-washing incident. I was not disciplined and admittedly enjoyed the applause when I returned to class that day. My understanding is Stephens had a heart-to-heart with the teacher, who, perhaps coincidentally, was not invited back to Eau Claire the next year.

The attention here, however, should not be about a smart-aleck teacher (or student) but about a coach who always was the epitome of integrity and honesty.

While times definitely have changed since the sixties, the world today certainly could benefit from more Art Bakers. And maybe a Paul Stephens.

Rest For Recliners

When our son Dalton married Leslie nearly 18 years ago, we booked a small Roswell band called "Banks and Shane" for the rehearsal party. The popular two-person band was outstanding, and a fun time was had by all.

Not too long ago, my WW and I decided our recliners needed a rest, so we took a look at the local entertainment lineup in our little town of Woodstock. Could it really be that "Banks and Shane" was playing at the MadLife Stage and Studios just a couple blocks away? Yes, and the only other question was whether to walk or drive.

After calling to reserve a high-top in the cozy balcony — our favorite perch at MadLife — we decided the cold and windy evening merited valet parking. After our two-minute drive, we were sitting comfortably at the high-top and watching as patrons filled the theater. It was an orderly crowd, and we looked down from the balcony to a sea of gray hair. This was going to be a really good night.

When Banks Burgess and Paul Shane took the stage, they did not look much different than 18 years ago. They had three band mates, but the focus almost always was on the group's namesakes, Banks the shorter of the two whose hair had changed from blonde to gray, and Shane, trimmer than in 2002 and still much taller than Banks. Banks warned the crowd quickly that everybody might want to take a swig of their stiff drinks so it would help them recognize the popular songs. But these two have not skipped a beat, so to speak, since they first started performing in 1972.

Old high school friends would have loved it. Jackie Downs, in particular, would have jumped up and led the shagging in the crowded spaces between the tables. Jackie could have won every shag contest since 1965 if she had a mind to, and this was vintage shagging by 70-something-year-olds who were re-living the good times of their lives and loving every minute of it.

After a hint of "Proud Mary" in the opener, the crowd joined in on "Sweet Caroline" and then went nuts with "Hunka, Hunka, Hunka Burning Love." Some songs just never get old. We weren't missing our recliners at this point. And why was it that I never learned to dance?

Banks and Shane sarcastically shared some details about their growing popularity and resulting notoriety. Like when they performed in a small Georgia town and were honored to crown the fruit cake queen whose name they could not remember. Which led straight into "What's Your Name…". One fun-loving fan nearly pulled a hamstring dancing to "Wake Up Little Susie" but settled down to "Dream, Dream, Dream."

Of course, these guys were absolutely spoofing about their notoriety. Since the rehearsal party for us 18 years ago, their popularity has skyrocketed. Their down home, southern act has carried them to Munich, Frankfurt, Amsterdam, and London as well as Georgia's governor's mansion for galas and inaugurations. They also opened for Alan Jackson although Shane likes to point out that "Alan Jackson actually closed for us."

My WW and I did not know what to expect after 18 years, but the young guy who valeted our car gave us a hint. "Banks and Shane? They were here earlier to warm up, and they actually sounded very good," he said as though he was surprised. Then again, this was a kid with tattoos who probably was born 18 years ago and had never even heard "Hang On Sloopy."

The show went by much too quickly. By the time "Wild Thing" and "Georgia On My Mind" were done, you would have thought the crowd—not to mention the band—would be ready for a break. No way. We still had several songs to go, including "Rocky Top Tennessee" and "Rock Me Mama." With time running out, Banks and Shane satisfied requests for some more shagging music, including "It's All Right" and "With This Ring" followed by "Build Me Up Buttercup."

By the time the band closed with "Desperado" and "Honky Tonk Blues" the crowd was howling for more. Had the MadLife theater schedule allowed, Banks and Shane likely would have obliged. It seemed they enjoyed the evening as much as their fatigued fans.

Thank goodness our recliners were waiting. They hadn't missed us. And vice versa.

Home

IT takes a heap o' livin' in a house t' make it home,
A heap o' sun an' shadder, an' ye sometimes have t' roam
Afore ye really 'preciate the things ye lef' behind,
An' hunger fer 'em somehow, with 'em allus on yer mind.
It don't make any differunce how rich ye get t' be,
How much yer chairs an' tables cost, how great yer luxury,
It ain't home t' ye, though it be the palace of a king,
Until somehow yer soul is sort o' wrapped round everything.

Home ain't a place that gold can buy or get up in a minute,
Afore it's home there's got t' be a heap o' livin' in it,
Within the walls there's got t' be some babies born, and then
Right there ye've got t' bring 'em up t' women good, an' men;
And gradjerly as time goes on, ye find ye wouldn't part
With anything they ever used -- they've grown into yer heart:
The old high chairs, the playthings, too, the little shoes they wore
Ye hoard; an' if ye could ye'd keep the thumb-marks on the door

Ye've got t' weep t' make it home, ye've got t' sit an' sigh
An' watch beside a loved one's bed, an' know that Death is nigh;
An' in the stillness o' the night t' see Death's angel come,
An' close the eyes o' her that smiled, an' leave her sweet voice dumb.
Fer these are scenes that grip the heart, an' when yer tears are dried,
Ye find the home is dearer than it was, an' sanctified;
An' tuggin' at ye always are the pleasant memories
O' her that was an' is no more -- ye can't escape from these.

Ye've got t' sing an' dance fer years, ye've got t' romp an' play,
An' learn t' love the things ye have by usin' 'em each day;
Even the roses 'round the porch must blossom year by year
Afore they 'come a part o' ye, suggestin' someone dear
Who used t' love 'em long ago, an' trained 'em jes t' run
The way they do, so's they would get the early mornin' sun;
Ye've got t' love each brick an' stone from cellar up t' dome:
It takes a heap o' livin' in a house t' make it home.

Edgar Guest

It Takes a Heap of Living

My elementary grade teacher had a thing for poetry. Mrs. Arndt. Back when putting the "r" in Mrs. did not offend anyone.

This poetry assignment was brutal. Memorize "Home" by Edgar A. Guest. Mrs. Arndt must have enjoyed torture. "Home" was not a four-liner. The first verse had almost 100 words and three other verses followed. Why in the world would any teacher inflict such agony on an elementary class?

And Mr. Guest did not make the assignment any easier. "Home" was written in a form of dialect that was difficult to read, much less memorize. The last two lines are a good example:

Ye've got t' love each brick an' stone from cellar up t' dome:
It takes a heap o' livin' in a house t' make it home.

Thank goodness Mrs. Arndt gave us a translated version to memorize with full words we could read and understand. But that made the assignment only slightly easier.

Why in the world? Why memorize a poem that most likely would be forgotten shortly after standing in front of classmates and embarrassing yourself as you try to recite the words?

I do recall we had several days to memorize the poem—mighty nice of Mrs. Arndt. I also remember getting totally frustrated in the evenings at home. I prayed Mrs. Arndt would be re-assigned the next day and the homework assignment would forever be forgotten. That did not happen.

So, I did the best I could, which was pretty good compared to some classmates who could not remember the name of the poem. On my day of reckoning, I made it through the first verse without much trouble. I did okay the rest of the way but needed prompting several times by Mrs. Arndt.

Well, to this day, 60-plus years later, I still remember most of the words.

It takes a heap of living in a house to make a home,
A heap of rain and sunshine and you sometimes have to roam,
Before you really appreciate the things you left behind,
With hunger for them always, with them always on your mind.

It took quite a few years, but the words have a much clearer meaning today. No doubt, Mrs. Arndt was preparing us for the future. A lot of truth to those first four lines, but you almost have to live your life to get the full meaning. The first two lines of each of the final three verses provide lessons of life yet to come for an elementary student:

Home ain't a place that gold can buy or get up in a minute;
Before it's home there's got to be a heap of living in it...
You've got to weep to make it home, you've got to sit and sigh

And watch beside a loved one's bed, and know that Death is nigh…
You've got to sing and dance for years, you've got to romp and play,
And learn to love the things you have by using them each day…

All the words following these opening lines carry meaningful messages of a perceptive poet. They would have been only words hidden in a book had it not been for an equally perceptive teacher.

Thank you, Edgar A. Guest. And thank you for the torture, Mrs. Arndt.

Four Lines

The elementary school homework assignment was simple: Write a four-line poem; turn it in tomorrow.

As I think back about 60 years, the teacher's name was Mrs. Gandy. Not absolutely sure about that, but no doubt the school was Heyward Gibbes, located mostly on Westwood Ave. with the main office on Summerlea Drive. The principal, no doubt, was C.A. Rampey, who lived on Westwood, across the street from the school.

Heyward Gibbes was spanking new back then. Elementary and middle school. Shiny cafeteria and classrooms and a gymnasium that was ruled by Frank Singleton. I can hear him now, "Hicky Duguley, don't you even think about going in that gym with your shoes on!" Coach Singleton often transposed the first letters of your first and last names to get your attention. At my 50-year high school reunion, he greeted me with, "Well, well, it's Hicky Duguley" before wrapping his big bear hug around me.

Interesting how those far away details can surface in a memory that sometimes cannot remember what was for lunch. Mrs. Shillinglaw taught music classes, my least favorite subject, at Heyward Gibbes. School basketball teams were divided into Midgets and Juniors—don't remember if those teams were based on body size or class. Girls, it seems, had to run only to the half-court line before giving up the basketball.

Miss Hiers was the young, good-looking history teacher with the pretty smile. She would be about 85 years old now. Mr. Wertz was the strict, no nonsense English teacher who drove everybody nuts with diagramming the longest sentences he could dream up. He later taught my daughter in middle school. Mrs. Strange taught math and was everyone's mother, a really nice lady.

Well, I digress accidentally on purpose. Heyward Gibbes was torn down and rebuilt years ago. Which means the bricks and mortar are gone but certainly not the memories. Which brings me back to that four-line poem. I just couldn't make it happen when I got home that day. But…

My Dad was a laborer who made a good living working hard every day as a plumber in my younger years. He came home totally tired every day. But I knew him for his humor and creative juices. I decided to ask him for help writing the four-line poem. His deal was for me to come up with my poem and he would try to come up with his, and then we would decide which one to use.

It was no contest. My Dad's poem was titled "Four Lines" and it became my poem and earned me an A for the homework assignment:

> *I've tried and tried just to see*
> *If a writer of poems I'll ever be.*
> *That's two lines and this is three,*
> *Now that I'm through I can watch TV.*

Some things you just never forget.

5. Church

My WW says it best. It doesn't really matter which church you go to as long as you go to church. As usual, she is right. I learned at an early age that if it's Sunday, your rear end needs to be parked in a pew. With your mouth closed and your ears open. And, if you go often enough, some of those sermons have messages that just might stick with you. Rev. Forrester once preached that there is no difference in a little white lie and a big black one. I've carried that nugget through life and still remember the look on his face when he said it.

I do believe I have sung "Amazing Grace" and "Just As I Am" at every church I've attended, and they just get better and better each time. And, I really don't know if I get more out of a Sunday service at an 8,000-strong congregation at Woodstock First Baptist or at a 17-strong congregation at Bethel United Methodist just up the road from The Cabin in middle Georgia. But it doesn't really matter which church you go to as long as you go.

Ridgecrest Baptist

Ridgecrest Baptist still stands on Abingdon Road in Columbia. Last time I drove by there, about three months ago, the small tree from the 60's on the front lawn had grown taller than the church, and a storm had broken it big time.

Everything about the church and its grounds looked shabby. The Laura Hollis Building needed some serious work, and the white block building at the back wasn't white anymore. My WW and I enjoyed our wedding reception in the Laura Hollis Building about 50 years ago. The block building housed the Sunday School nursery back in the old days, and the RA's and GA's met there, too. That's Royal Ambassadors and Girls Auxiliary for those who forget.

The Laura Hollis Building was the church sanctuary until the sparkling new church was built right next to it. Deacons would remove a portion of the Hollis Building floor so baptisms could take place there in a pit. Eerie back then. We used mostly folding chairs for worship services in the Hollis Building. Afterwards, we would walk next door through the construction mess to see how much progress had been made the previous week on the new church. I thought it would never be finished.

Ridgecrest was an active and thriving church back in the 60's. Reverend Vello Forrester was the pastor, and the church had many families in leadership roles. This could cause trouble because of omissions, but I'll name a few: the Hedgepaths, McCaws, Crofts, Kalutzes, Lybrands, Readys, Millers, Belfords, Lyons, Hedgepaths, Elkins and even a family with the last name of Church. Many with the same names anchored the church on the board of deacons year after year. They cut and raked the grounds when needed, prepared food for gatherings, set up the Hollis Building for weddings and receptions, taught classes, and volunteered time for youth outings.

Sunday School was vibrant and included Bible drills for youngsters: *Attention!… Draw Swords (Bibles)… Find… Matthew 28:19-20; Matthew 28:19-20… Ready… Charge!* And the flurry of pages turning began until someone stepped forward with fingers on the designated scripture. Locating lesser-known books like Ezekiel or Amos or Micah was always difficult. The New Testament was not as challenging except for a couple like Titus or Philemon.

Morning worship services were marked by families sitting together and usually on the same pew week after week. And it wasn't a legitimate service without Annie Nungezer at the organ. The evening service was preceded by Training Union, mostly a good excuse for young people to socialize while at church and afterwards. Mid-week Prayer Meetings were held every Wednesday evening, sparsely attended but a good platform for more social activities for young people. And prayers, many times long, long, sleep-inducing prayers. Seems like Mr. Ready was the longest-winded, but others weren't far behind.

Even though I could not sing a lick, music from the Baptist Hymnal was enjoyable. Favorites included any song by the official church trio of Myrtice Miller, Evelyn Kalutz, and Thelma Dugosh; a solo of The King's Business by Ernest Miller, whose bass voice was deeper than the Hollis Building baptismal pool; and, any song by big John Jones, a round music director who sat on the dais but could not stay awake for an entire service. Before services would begin, friends would try to guess the time his eyes would close and his head nod. One of us would cough or clear our throat to see if we could jolt Big John awake and then try our best not to laugh. All of this, of course, while taking in Rev. Forrester's message.

My cousin Bill once visited Ridgecrest with me. It was a Sunday morning service and the invitational hymn, which comes at the end of Baptist services, was "Just As I Am." I do believe Ridgecrest sometimes extended the invitation—and continued to sing verse after verse—until someone came forward to join or re-commit their life. Well, Cousin Bill, not necessarily sound spiritually back then, was astonished after at least a dozen verses of "Just As I Am." "I was ready to walk the aisle myself," he said, but not for the right reason.

Homecoming Sunday was another highlight at Ridgecrest. Former members, present members, and prospective members converged at the corner of Abingdon and Hillcrest for normally the largest congregation of the year. I always suspected that people came mostly for the food—many, many covered dishes that always included too few deviled eggs but plenty of fried chicken and desserts.

The vibrant church began to wane as the neighborhood started to disperse to the suburbs, primarily to the growing St. Andrews area. Many members commuted for years before moving their memberships, and the next generation and the next were not as committed. Growth leveled off and then began to decline, a familiar trend for many community churches. What remains is a shabby shadow of a once-proud community church.

When I took a right turn off Duke Avenue three months ago, I was anxious and apprehensive about what might be ahead. One block up on the left was Ridgecrest Baptist and the dingy Laura Hollis Building. The huge oak, planted shortly after the new sanctuary was dedicated, was broken and splintered. With no deacons to clean it up.

I took a picture that day but will not publish it. I'd rather Ridgecrest Baptist be remembered as the vibrant church of the 1960's that touched many lives.

Sunday Morning Left Turn

We were on our way to church one Sunday several years ago. We had moved to Woodstock from Roswell a year earlier, so the drive to Roswell Presbyterian was a lengthy 35 minutes or more. Of course, we were running late and had left ourselves about 20 minutes to get there. Which meant we would not make it for the music, which many times was the most uplifting part of the service for me.

My WW always was better at listening to the minister's message than me; my mind tends to wander to much less important subjects—like where we would go for lunch, when could I get to The Cabin again, were the Braves going to win, or how in the world our national politicians have managed to royally screw things up so badly. But I digress.

So, we were not going to make it to Roswell Presbyterian anywhere near on time, and we were passing the huge Woodstock Baptist campus. Why not give it a try? A quick left turn and we were in a humongous parking lot—and it was only for senior citizens and limited mobility folks. And it was completely full. Regular attendees were being shuttled from more distant lots. We looked like lost sinners, so the volunteers in bright orange vests waved us into the visitor parking area.

We found our way to the main sanctuary in time for the opening hymn. What looked like a 200-person choir bellowed the words of "Just As I Am" as we found our seats in this massive indoor stadium. I had not heard "Just As I Am" at church since my teenage years at Ridgecrest Baptist in Columbia, S.C. And as I listened to the singing, I wondered if this left-turn decision was one of those divine intervention moments.

I would have been mesmerized by the sheer size of everything inside Woodstock Baptist had it not been for the pastor and his ability to captivate the congregation. Who was this unmasked man? Johnny Hunt. Not The Reverend or Most Honorable. Just Johnny.

I had seen Johnny Hunt's name on a road sign—for some reason a major thoroughfare in front of the church had been named for him. After hearing him, I understood why. But he looked sort of ordinary. No suit, no white shirt, not even a tie. But this man could preach The Word—perhaps even better than Rev. Vello Forrester, my boyhood pastor at Ridgecrest, who often admonished us all that "There is no difference in a little white lie and a big black one." True stuff.

But Johnny Hunt's background is stunning: a reformed drinker and gambler from a shady pool hall life with a message that was, and is, unmistakable and a commitment that was, and is, crystal clear. He is a man of God. Minds do not wander when he is delivering his messages. Not even mine.

Absolutely nothing against Roswell Presbyterian, but we no longer make that 35-minute drive to Roswell except when our granddaughters are in a special program. And the left turn that Sunday morning added to an interesting dichotomy in our lives. When in Woodstock, we attend a church of 8,000 with a $17 million budget. When in middle Georgia at The Cabin, we attend a church of 20-something where members pool their Christmas cards and send them to us in one envelope to save postage. Bethel United Methodist is the mid-Georgia rural jewel where people experience real life. When the church needs money, members are apt to schedule a series of yard sales. Their prayer request list is much longer than its membership roll. Johnny Hunt would love that little church.

And we love Woodstock Baptist. Divine intervention? Surely glad we made that left turn years ago.

The Beauty of Bethel

Attendance was good on this particular Sunday. Up a couple to 19.

Bethel United Methodist Church, situated on Highway 212 in middle Georgia and established in 1813, had fourteen in attendance the previous week, according to the chart on the wall, which meant several regulars must have been sick. Members at Bethel don't miss unless they are not able.

And if you should become ill, you're apt to get well in a hurry with this group of prayer warriors working for you. The prayer request list always is lengthy and comprehensive. One

Sunday we prayed for Gerald's injured finger. Bethel doesn't miss much.

That's just one part of the beauty of Bethel, and that's why my WW and I have visited for twenty-three years. If we're at The Cabin on a Sunday, we'll be sitting in our regular pew place come 10 a.m. It's the same pew place where Bethel leaves our Christmas cards until we can get back for them.

Bethel's cookouts and picnics are special. Hank usually takes charge. "Here, sprinkle some of this seasoning on your plate and then just roll your corn on the cob in it; it will taste even better," he suggests. And he was right. Not a better place to learn about the people who make up Bethel than while sitting around a table at one of these gatherings.

There's Gerald who loves to visit Alaska, but he doesn't want to fly or cruise. So, he drives. "I guess it's about 5,000 miles," he said. And he's done it several times. Gerald and wife Polly always sit in front of us. Same spot every Sunday. And there's Dee and Doug who always settle four rows from the front on the right. Dee and Doug assume responsibility for sending out birthday and anniversary cards and any announcements to Bethel members and visitors, and they also take care of the church's financial matters.

Then there's Mr. Al, owner and operator of Haslam's Marina on Lake Sinclair since 1961. His Sunday spot is the second row, left side, near the aisle. Mr. Al is a walking encyclopedia of everything community, Lake Sinclair, and Bethel United Methodist Church. Church services seem more official with the World War II Navy veteran sitting in his spot.

And Louis and Eleanor, a few rows from the front on the left side, are always good for a handshake and a hug, respectively. Among Louis' duties at Bethel is passing the offering plate each Sunday.

Rev. Terry plays a key role in this band of Christians. He rides a Methodist circuit that takes him to two churches every Sunday and three churches at least once a month. The other churches are small, he points out. Yes, smaller than Bethel. When he's not preaching, he's teaching … eighth-grade special education students. Rev. Terry also occasionally brings his bass guitar to liven up the church music. And, Kim, one of the pianists, also teaches special ed. So does Judy—second row, right side—a Bethel attendee for 20-plus years.

All are examples of the beauty of Bethel where members and visitors always stand together in support of one another, especially during challenging times. The little church on the hill with its aging congregation faces the reality of thinning out. While Rev. Terry's message from the pulpit on a recent Sunday focused on Jeremiah, one of his mini messages was a nugget for this maturing congregation: messengers may pass away but not their messages.

Bethel United Methodist has been sending messages since 1813. Larger congregations have come and gone over the years, but numbers on a wall chart can have sparse meaning. This little church on Highway 212 remains vibrant in its own way. It has more heart than numbers.

That's the real beauty of Bethel.

Godly Intervention at The Way

The small sanctuary oozed tradition. Old hymnals. Wooden pews. Paper bulletins. Collection plates. A mostly gray-haired congregation. Beautiful soft hymns. And Pastor Ann wore a robe.

Not far away, maybe a mile, was another church. Not totally opposite the much older one but nearly. Assembled in a rental property. Fold-up chairs rather than pews. A praise band with guitars and drums. Not much gray hair if any. And Pastor Andy wore jeans.

Woodstock United Methodist Church, the one steeped in tradition with the pristine sanctuary, had approximately 25 loyal attendees on a good Sunday. The nearby church, also United Methodist, was named City On A Hill. It had a membership roll of 200-plus.

And, yes, there's Ann and Andy. Not the raggedy dolls but the unlikely couple with a vision.

These two churches would appear to have little in common other than Methodist doctrine. There was no way for the two to think about merging. No way. The two congregations were reflections of their ministers: the mature, traditional Ann and the youthful, contemporary Andy. But Ann and Andy themselves had a vision that sidelined any differences, and their hearts were identical. Plus, the churches needed each other.

City On A Hill had the people, was outgrowing its facilities, and was nearing the end of an expensive lease. Woodstock United Methodist had the facilities but not the people, and the future was anything but robust. But the doll duo—Ann and Andy—had the spirit and the vision.

So, the seed was planted for bringing the two churches together. It was not without disagreement—and even dissension—at times. Long-time stalwarts at WUMC wanted little to do with drums and electric guitars in their revered sanctuary, and the younger COAH crowd wasn't sure it could sit still for "Just As I Am."

But then God intervened. People in both congregations started to dip their toes in compromise and understanding as members began to accept that their theme of Better Together indeed was better. Lo and behold, even Covid restrictions could not keep this vision from coming into focus. My goodness, Andy even wore a robe every now and then... with jeans beneath.

Probably the most anxious time in the transition related to an early decision that neither of the churches' names would be retained once the merger was complete. The older folks at WUMC could not fathom giving up a shingle that had hung for 150 years, and the COAH congregation took tremendous pride in its name as well. But there could be no compromise on this point—an absolute condition of the merger by both parties was that neither name would remain.

And then God intervened. After considerable study and prayer, a committee with equal representation presented the new name: The Way Woodstock—A United Methodist Church.

For a while, it seemed there was no way this merger was going to work. But then there was, almost suddenly, The Way.

Proof of success at The Way does not come in finances or facilities. Ann and Andy regularly emphasize what's most important: the number of souls who come to Christ. Practical steps are being taken at The Way that suggest continuing success toward this ultimate goal. A capital building campaign has an appropriate name in "Making Room" with impressive results; and traditional and contemporary services are in place now that Covid restrictions have eased, which means traditional and contemporary music offerings each Sunday.

"Making Room" improvements will allow the guitars and drums to retreat eventually from the sanctuary, and their new digs will mean a better setting for more vibrant music and modern services that are popular among today's youth. And young people today are tomorrow's future.

And something even better is happening without a whole lot of notice. The not-so-gray worshippers have been sliding into the sanctuary pews recently, singing along, and obviously enjoying, the old hymns and piano-only accompaniment. Who knows, maybe some of the gray-haired bunch just might sneak into the contemporary service and enjoy blending with the not-so-gray worshippers and join in on the toe tapping.

Talk about Godly intervention.

6. Career

I knew what I didn't want to be before I knew what I wanted to be.

It was my first day as a plumber's helper at a school construction site. My boss was my dad. "I want you to dig a ditch from this corner of the yard to that corner. Six inches deep and four to six inches wide. I'll be back to check on you."

It was summertime hot, and the ground was rock hard, but I did not want to disappoint on my very first assignment. After three hours, I was about halfway to the other corner. It took five hours for the other half. I was soaked in sweat and had plenty of blisters. "Good job," my dad said. "Now, let's go home." I wondered if we were going to put pipe in the ditch, but my dad said, "No, we'll cover up this ditch tomorrow." But… "I just wanted you to see what you didn't want to do for the rest of your life," he said simply. He might not have finished high school, but my dad was a pretty good teacher.

So, I learned what I didn't want to do. But what did I want to do?

An Idea for A Career

I really wanted to be a sportswriter. How neat it would be to get paid to watch games.

Encouraged by high school teacher and journalism coach

Rachel Haynie, I decided to put in an application at The Columbia Record newspaper in Columbia, S.C. This part of the process did not excite me at all, but I saw it as a necessary evil.

The security guard motioned me in and toward the receptionist at the State-Record building across from the fairgrounds. The receptionist said I should go to the Personnel Department—elevator to the second floor and take a right. Instead, I took a left off the elevator after seeing "Sports Department" on a sign. This was 1966 when I did not have a lot of courage in such situations. But I really wanted to be a sportswriter.

The gruff guy behind the sports desk didn't want to be bothered. Jim Hunter's reputation as sports editor was almost frightening. He kind of growled at me, "What you need?" Then, "The Personnel Department is down the hall."

The Personnel Department wasn't any cheerier. No greeting. No smiles. "Fill out this application, put it in the top tray, and we'll contact you." Which I did. The top tray, however, must have had a hundred applications stacked up. At least mine would be on top. "Put it on the bottom," the clerk said. "The bottom." No smile. No thank you.

I knew I was getting nowhere fast. But I really wanted to be a sportswriter.

I would settle for being at the bottom of the totem pole on any sports staff. Happy to take the crummy assignments. Did not have to cover the mighty Eau Claire Shamrocks or Lower Richland Diamond Hornets and certainly not the USC Gamecocks or Clemson. Give me the assignments nobody wanted; but give me an assignment.

I had noticed in the sports department a sheet tacked to the bulletin board. It was staff assignments for high school football games for Thursday and Friday nights as well as for Saturday's college games. The Personnel Department experience was frustrating, but I decided not to give up. I had an idea…

I went to Memorial Stadium that Thursday evening, sat in the stands and watched the Dreher-Camden high school football game. Notepad and pen in hand, I took notes just like a legitimate sportswriter. After the game, I told the security guard at the field gate that I was a sportswriter and needed to talk to Earl Rankin, the Dreher coach. I waved my notepad at the guard, who, thankfully, fell for my bluff and waved me onto the field. Coach Rankin saw my notepad, stopped at midfield, and answered a couple of my questions. I was an imposter.

All of that was the easy part. I drove all the way back to my home in the Eau Claire part of town, penciled out a short story on the game, typed it with a carbon paper copy, and then drove back to the State-Record building. It was after midnight. Then the really risky part. I sort of lied (there's no such thing) to the security guard at the entrance to the building. Walked right past him, waving the story and mumbling "Gotta make deadline." I fumbled for an ID badge that I did not have, and the guard said, "Just don't worry about it." Whew!

Of course, I knew the way to the deserted sports department. Clicked on a light, plopped the typed story on Jim Hunter's desk with a note: "Use this if you'd like; no charge." I thanked the security guard on my way out of the building. Little did he know…

The next afternoon, Friday's Columbia Record sports section included a small story, boxed on the front sports page, about the Dreher-Camden football game at Memorial Stadium. I did not get paid for my first published story, but I did get an unexpected bonus — my first byline.

The next week, the assignment sheet tacked to the bulletin board included a rookie part-time staffer who was assigned two high school games. Soon it was two high school games and two college games every week. I couldn't get enough of it.

I was a sportswriter.

Short Trip of a Lifetime

In 1974, I had two suits. Actually, only one. The navy-blue sports coat didn't really count as a suit, but I could wear it with a tie and gray pants or khaki pants.

So, I carefully packed both suits, several pairs of slacks, several ties, both pairs of shoes I owned, including my Bass Weejuns, all my dress shirts including my prized blue Gant, and all the underwear and socks I owned. This was going to be the trip of a lifetime, and I was excited.

Doug Nye, Sports Editor of The Columbia Record, had given me the plum assignment of any sportswriter's career: go to Atlanta and follow the Atlanta Braves and Hank Aaron until Aaron breaks Babe Ruth's home run record. Absolutely the top thrill of my young career.

I certainly wanted to be prepared so I bought one of those bars for hanging clothes from window to window in the back seat. No telling how long I would be gone. My WW made sure my toiletry bag was fully stocked, and my closet was depleted as I loaded the family Ford Torino.

Of course, this was going to be work so I did my homework. It was the beginning of the 1974 major league baseball season and the Braves had opened the season with three games in Cincinnati. It did not matter that the Braves lost two of those games because Aaron hit a home run in his first at-bat of the season to tie Babe Ruth's record of 714 career home runs. Atlanta bigwigs wanted Aaron to break the coveted record in Atlanta, and Aaron went the final two games in Cincinnati without another home run, which set the stage perfectly for Atlanta fans. And I couldn't wait to get to Atlanta.

I pulled my Torino into the parking garage at the Intercontinental Hotel across the street from Fulton County Stadium. I needed a cart with wheels to tote my clothes to my room, and the nice hotel bell captain offered his assistance. He mentioned I had lots of clothes, and I told him I would be staying until Aaron hits THE home run. He flashed a wide smile as I rushed to check in and get to the stadium.

It was more than 47 years ago, but the details are crystal clear.

The Braves public relations staff had prepared an impressive information package for members of the press. A "Hank Aaron Media Guide" included every statistic imaginable, including a list of Aaron's 714 home runs with information on EACH home run including the date, inning it was hit, number of runners on base, the opposing team, and the opposing pitcher.

The same statistics were included for each of Ruth's 714 homers as well. A 47-page report on George Herman "Babe" Ruth was included in the package. The report noted that Ruth, who died in 1948, was known as "The Sultan of Swat," "The Bambino," "The King of Clout," "The Colossus of Rhodes," "The Mighty Maharaja of Maul," and "The Caliph of Clout." Aaron, an unassuming sports hero, was known simply as "Hammerin' Hank."

Like me, the city of Atlanta was totally pumped up, and a sellout crowd of 53,000 was on hand that evening, April 8 of 1974, when the Braves returned home to play the Dodgers. I had a catbird seat on press row, just above the lower deck on the first-base side. Perfect view of the batter's box and the field.

Dodger pitcher Al Downing did not want to be stigmatized as the pitcher who gave up the record-breaking home run. He walked Hammerin' Hank in the first inning as the 53,000 roared with boos. The first strike he threw Aaron came in the fourth inning, and it was hammered over the left field fence and into the glove of bullpen relief pitcher Tommy House. The wait for 715 was over, and Aaron was the king of baseball.

Not many of the 53,000 were in the stadium at the end to see the Braves win the game 7-4. They had seen what they came to see, and they had been part of baseball history. Many of them surely would tell their grandchildren about being there that night.

I could not get enough of the occasion. With press credentials, I was allowed in the Braves locker room with gobs of other sports writers after the game. Aaron sat nonchalantly on a bench in front of his locker. He was calm and obviously relieved. He said the same words many times: "I'm just glad it's over."

Sports writers eventually filtered out of the locker room and left Aaron with his closest friends and members of the Braves organization. I stuck around as long as I could, actually too long. When I left the locker room, I realized I was locked inside the stadium. A security guard told me one gate was still open on the other side of the stadium but I should hurry. After hustling to the one open gate, I no longer had to worry about spending the night in Fulton County Stadium.

I walked across the street to the hotel and fell asleep long after midnight. The next morning, I packed up all my clothes, put everything on one of those carts with wheels, and headed down the elevator. "Didn't need all those clothes, did you?" the bell captain quipped with his wide smile.

My two suits and I were back on I-20 toward Columbia after less than 24 hours in Atlanta. As I drove back home, I thought to myself, the trip of a lifetime was short, but maybe my children and grandchildren will like hearing about it someday.

Grandad, Are You Old?

One of my grandchildren, sitting on my lap some time ago, was staring at me before innocently asking, "Grandad, are you old?"

"Goodness, no," I replied. "I'm just an old timer."

Which, crazily, led me to think about the Old Timers Game in Atlanta, 1975. And, a prized possession, the picture of me and Joe DiMaggio together in a dugout at now demolished

Fulton County Stadium. DiMaggio, popularly known as Joltin' Joe and The Yankee Clipper, is still considered one of the best major league players of all time. The picture, neatly framed by my WW, sits on a shelf in a corner of my office; I call it my ego corner and that picture is the centerpiece. The camera also caught DiMaggio's trademark tip of his hat when I handed him a baseball to sign. A sportswriter from Sumter, S.C., snapped the picture and mailed it to me weeks later. I did not know he took it, and I could not thank him enough.

The 1975 Old Timers Game featured a lot of former baseball stars. They were "former" even back in 1975. Most have dozed off and woke up in heaven, as I would tell my grandkids.

Joe DiMaggio, Red Schoendienst, Pee Wee Reese, Hoyt Wilhelm, Larry Doby, Ralph Branca, Luke Appling, Johnny Vander Meer — they were all there. They are all together today, probably playing catch in baseball heaven. With them upstairs is Bill Skowron, Ken Boyer, Bob Turley, Tito Francona, and several others who played in that three-inning game 43 years ago. I know of only two who are still awake here on earth — Bill Mazeroski and Bobby Richardson.

Being on the field with these greats — prior to the actual game, of course — was unforgettable. This might be boring stuff unless you are a baseball buff. If you are into baseball, you might know that Pittsburgh's Mazeroski hit a home run in the bottom of the ninth inning in the 1960 World Series to beat the Yankees (and Richardson).

And Richardson — from Sumter, S.C. and a former University of South Carolina baseball coach—set a major league record with six runs batted in against the Pirates in one game in that same World Series. That record still stands although it has been tied by two other players.

The other Old Timers were quite distinguished, too, probably more so. DiMaggio, of course, had at least one hit in 56 consecutive games, a record that still stands in the major leagues. Most baseball experts say that record never will be broken. Pitcher Vander Meer had back-to-back no-hitters for the Cincinnati Reds, a feat never equaled. Ken Boyer had a grand slam in the 1964 World Series that highlighted the Cardinals' series win over the Yankees. And, so on … if they had not accomplished something truly remarkable, they would not have been honored as an Old Timer that day.

It was Richardson who was the star among stars in the 1975 Old Timers Game, not that it mattered. My much-faded play-by-play notes, now 46 years old, show that he opened the game with a single on the first pitch, stole second, and later scored. He also scored after a double in the third inning, and his team won the abbreviated game 3-1. And that didn't matter either.

What mattered was baseball fans had a chance to see some of the all-time greats of the game. Most are no longer are here, and memories of them have faded, but the Old Timers enjoyed being there for their fans in the twilight of their lives.

I know because it takes an Old Timer to know an Old Timer.

Atlanta? No Way

I could not think of a single reason to leave Columbia. Plus, there were plenty of reasons to stay.

The year was 1987. My WW and I were snug with three children in a nice West Columbia home. Each of the kids was getting ready to change schools—one starting elementary, one moving up to a nearby middle school, and the other leaving that middle school for her first year of high school.

My Dad had recently passed away, and I had moved my mother close to us. We had wonderful friends in all walks of life. My career in the newspaper business was promising. The overused quip was applicable: Life is good.

Then the phone rang. I was out of the office the first three times, and each time the written message noted a call from "Buddy Ward in Atlanta." Probably an investment guy, so I did not return any of his calls. On the fourth occasion, before caller ID, I answered the ring myself.

Buddy Ward was president of Atlanta Newspapers. Wanted to talk about my coming to work there. It was a quick "No" from me. He persisted. "Listen," I told him politely, "I have everything right here in Columbia that anyone could want. No interest in moving anywhere."

No way we were moving to Atlanta. No way.

Buddy then asked if I would visit Atlanta, meet some folks, and think about it. Politely but "No" again. But he did not give up. If he drove to Columbia, would I at least have lunch with him? This guy was nice but really hard-headed.

I agreed to the lunch but told him he would be wasting his time.

A couple days later at lunch, his opener was, "You sure are hard-headed." We had a good laugh. I told him I could not imagine uprooting my family, leaving friends and everything else after living almost all my life in Columbia, not to mention 21 years at Columbia Newspapers. He said he certainly understood. "But," he added, "now you owe me a trip to Atlanta. And bring your family."

Of course, my WW and I talked a lot about all of this. I didn't think she wanted to leave Columbia, putting the children in a new world, giving up a lot for a change of life in a big city. Not to mention Atlanta traffic. Did Columbia even have cars back in '87? No, there was no way we were moving. No way.

But we did decide to take up Buddy on his invitation to visit. We rationalized it as a mini-vacation on Atlanta Newspapers' tab.

Our Atlanta hotel reservation was made by Atlanta Newspapers, Inc. It included a very large suite. On the table in the foyer was a huge arrangement of flowers for my WW. And a big fruit basket for the family. And jerseys and jackets for the kids — amazingly with the correct sizes for each. And Braves and Falcons hats and all sorts of goodies for the kids.

Nice try, but still there was no way we were moving to Atlanta. No way.

After meeting the newspaper's general manager and having a nice dinner, his single request was that I plan a return visit, meet other key folks at the newspaper and then make a decision. Just think about it. No pressure.

We figured out the interstates and battled the Atlanta traffic to get back to Columbia. The ride home was scary silent at times. The key for us always has been good people. We knew Columbia had many good people, and we had met two obviously good Atlanta Newspapers people. But there was no way we were moving to Atlanta. Not a chance.

Out of courtesy, we decided that I should return to Atlanta one more time to close out this discussion personally.

So, I returned to Atlanta and met several others at the newspapers. Afterwards, back in Columbia, I told my WW that obviously there are good people in Atlanta, too. We agreed to think about things overnight, but then I would call Buddy Ward with our official decision to stay in Columbia.

I remember not sleeping that night. The next morning, I needed to hear from WW. Without hesitation, she said, "I think we should do it."

No way we were going to Atlanta. No way.

Been here 34 years.

Blog Number 50

After submitting 49 blogs for *A Little Piece of Heaven*, I asked my publisher to stop the presses. I thought it would be neat for this book to have a tidy 50 blogs. So, what about blog number 50?

Should I write about the Terrible Twenty, a golf outing years ago in North Carolina, and friend Dennis, who also happens to be the best leader I worked with during my career?

Or should it be about Fay, one of the best moms ever who drove away from Publix without her groceries … and kids? Fay also has a twin sister Gay. Fay didn't really go up to a stranger in a restaurant and ask, "You must think I'm Gay." Did she?

Or maybe it should be about Tom, Dick and, finally, Harry. Susie and Debbie interrupted my parents' plans.

Perhaps my experiences at Fantasy Camp with the Atlanta Braves. That's where approximately 75 percent of participants pull a hamstring before their first game and cannot play.

Or a more somber tone about when a dad dies and why old guys cry so much.

Or about The Talent Pyramid, my way of explaining to my children why they are cut from sports teams.

Or a blog about young granddaughters who play golf with Grandad.

Perhaps a piece about being senior speaker at my high school graduation and now a senior speaker at age three-quarters of a century.

Another possibility is a blog about heroes and angels … like my sister Debbie, my publisher Bob, Gwen, or my WW.

Maybe the blog should be about three friends of my youth who are gone — Danny, Jim and Ernie — and what I had to say about them at their funerals.

Or something about my neighbors at The Cabin, somewhat opposites Bill and Paul. You didn't think The Cabin would be left out, did you?

Somewhere inside me just might be a blog about cousin Bill and how he has navigated this world.

Or brother Harry, who is somewhere in the mountains of Montana with a story of his own to tell.

Perhaps a blog about buying our move-in ready home in Woodstock, but taking four months to get it ready to move in.

I know there's a blog in me about the letters I wrote to each of my three children as they left home for college.

Or one about the late Frank Singleton—coach, teacher, boxer, mentor, all-everything to everybody who knew him—and the friend who hung "Hicky Duguley" on me.

Or a blog about five couples, friends since grammar school, who gather to celebrate Golden anniversaries together this year.

Maybe some musings about our family Christmases at Waffle House and letters from Santa.

I think I just finished blog number 50.

I might have to publish another book.

About the Author

Dick has loved writing all of his life. He worked his way through college as a sports writer at *The Columbia Record* newspaper. In 1987 he became Vice President of Circulation at *The Atlanta Journal/Constitution* and moved from Columbia to Atlanta. In 2002 he became VP for Development for Cox Enterprises, Inc., owners of the AJC. He retired in 2008 after 42 years that included twin 21-year careers in Columbia and Atlanta. Although his executive career pulled him away from writing, he always knew he would return to it. He began writing and publishing blogs via Facebook and published 38 blogs in 2018-2019. *A Little Piece of Heaven* is a culmination of both his published and unpublished blogs.